"This book is theologically sound, pastorally insightful, grounded in Christ, and rooted in Scripture. Helpful tools and ways of giving voice to the dying and to their loved ones are provided for the church's ministry."

—**Abigail Rian Evans**, PhD, LHD, Center for Clinical Bioethics, Georgetown University Medical Center; Princeton Seminary

"Christians often say they are not afraid of death—it's the process of dying that raises anxiety. *Speaking of Dying* lays a solid biblical and theological foundation connecting baptism and the Eucharist to their fulfillment in death, which aids our understanding of how dying 'in Christ' is counter to the cultural milieu of avoidance. The authors encourage pastors and congregational members to speak of their dying both to strengthen their faith and to receive support. This theological road map will most definitely enhance the reader's approach to a dying person."

—**Susan J. Zonnebelt-Smeenge**, RN, EdD, licensed clinical psychologist, and **Robert C. DeVries**, DMin, PhD, pastor and emeritus professor at Calvin Theological Seminary

"This book is a wonderful contribution to restoring the sacred art of facing the end of life. It is a deep and reflective analysis of the culture of dying and the Christian experience of living and dying, and a valuable resource for theologians, health care professionals, and all who seek to honor the final chapter of life."

—**Betty Ferrell**, PhD, FAAN, FPCN, CHPN, City of Hope Medical Center, Duarte, CA

Speaking of Dying

RECOVERING THE CHURCH'S VOICE
IN THE FACE OF DEATH

FRED CRADDOCK,
DALE GOLDSMITH, AND JOY V. GOLDSMITH

Brazos Press

a division of Baker Publishing Group
Grand Rapids, Michigan

Published by Brazos Press
a division of Baker Publishing Group
P.O. Box 6287, Grand Rapids, MI 49516-6287
www.brazospress.com

Printed in the United States of America

Library of Congress Cataloging-in-Publication Data
Craddock, Fred B.
    Speaking of dying : recovering the church's voice in the face of death / Fred Craddock, Dale Goldsmith, and Joy V. Goldsmith.
        p.   cm.
    Includes bibliographical references (p.   ) and index.
    ISBN 978-1-58743-323-8 (pbk.)
    1. Death—Religious aspects—Christianity. I. Goldsmith, Dale. II. Goldsmith, Joy V. III. Title.
    BT825.C73 2012
    236'.1—dc23   ·   2012000803

12   13   14   15   16   17   18   7   6   5   4   3   2   1

In keeping with biblical principles of creation stewardship, Baker Publishing Group advocates the responsible use of our natural resources. As a member of the Green Press Initiative, our company uses recycled paper when possible. The text paper of this book is composed in part of post-consumer waste.

Because of Rev. Janet Forts Goldsmith (1968–2002)—our daughter, sister, student

Contents

Tables

Foreword

They had not expected him to die. He was in the critical-care unit of the hospital in a city some distance from where they lived, so they knew he was very sick. But they did not think he was going to die anytime soon. They traveled to see him, assuming that he would at least for a time get better. As soon as they walked into his room in the hospital, however, it was clear he was dying. The struggle he faced helped those who loved him to recognize that the medical interventions were only prolonging the inevitable.

Moreover, he was being forced to breathe, making impossible any communication between him and his family. If a nurse had not been present to help the family understand that he was suffering from an illness from which he would not recover, he would have died without interacting with his family. The intervention of the nurse made it possible for his therapy to be revised, which meant he could receive the love of his family, family members could pray for him, and he knew he would not die alone. He soon died, surrounded by those who represented how his story reflected a Christian life.

I was a witness to this death. It was not long after my involvement with this death that I was asked to write the foreword to

Speaking of Dying. Reading through the book, I could only think how much it is needed given what I had just witnessed. There is simply no question that too often we lack the words necessary to speak to one another about dying and death. Death threatens speech, often reducing us to silence. There can be a silence whose eloquence is a form of prayer, but too often the silence surrounding death is little more than noisy platitudes we are not sure are even true. "He or she is in a better place" tries to comfort, but it does so by denying the reality of death itself.

As the authors of this book document through paying close attention to the lives of ministers who are dying, it seems that Christians have lost our ability to "speak of dying" with one another. The essential story—the story of the life, death, and resurrection of Christ—that should form our dying as well as our living as Christians seems to have been lost. The authors no doubt are right to suggest that the way our dying has become the province of medicine may be one of the reasons Christians have lost our ability to speak of death. That another procedure always seems possible too often results in a person dying without being able to have his or her dying storied by the story of the church. It would be a mistake, however, to blame those associated with medicine for this result. As the authors make clear, Christians have only themselves to blame for losing the story that should make it possible to speak of death.

Take, for example, something as simple and significant as where the funeral is to take place. The authors rightly note that this is not a book about funerals; however, funerals often reflect how we have or have not learned to speak about death. The person whose death I witnessed had left instructions for his funeral to take place in a funeral home. As a result, the liturgy was less than it should have been, and it failed to reflect his many years of faithful attendance at his church. Somehow he had not been formed by the church to recognize the relationship between his baptism and his death. So those gathered at his funeral became an audience rather than a congregation.

I am, perhaps, particularly sensitive to the connection between baptism and the funeral because of the practice of my church. We have a cross-shaped baptismal that is sufficiently large to immerse not only children but adults. When one of our members dies, the coffin is placed on the baptismal the night before the funeral. We then take turns keeping vigil with our dead brother or sister through the night until the funeral is held. The connection so established between baptism and the funeral has made it possible for the church to speak about death in quite remarkable ways.

I am not suggesting that this church always gets it right, but rather I am calling attention to the fact that the small act of displaying the connection between baptism and death turns out to be one of the most significant defining characteristics of this church. This simple action seems to have unleashed the kind of speech this book suggests we desperately need if we are to speak truthfully of death. As these authors argue, the death of Jesus means Christians have a storied death that enables us to speak to one another about our dying. It may well be, therefore, that one of the most determinative witnesses Christians can make in our time is to be a people who know how to speak of dying.

Particularly noteworthy is the authors' suggestion that Christians have the psalms of lament as a resource to shape our dying. These authors rightly distance themselves from those who attempt to make death a spiritual experience. Drawing on Arthur McGill's great work on death, they remind us that we cannot experience our own deaths, but we can recognize that we need to die in order to discover our true selves. Therefore, death is properly lamented, but also celebrated as new life.

This is a book we have desperately needed. I hope it will become a book widely studied in congregations and seminaries. We must learn to speak of dying. This book appropriately helps us recover our voices as a people taught to speak by the one who died on a cross.

Stanley Hauerwas

Preface

I selfishly claim to have known my sister better than anyone else did. She was a pastor, and in her desperate time of degradation and loss—in the midst of a congregation and governing body unable to engage the subject of her dying constructively—I observed a train wreck. The experience changed my entire life. I turned from an academic career in the theatre to the world of uncertainty, anxiety, and fear heard in the communication of dying patient to caregiver, dying patient to clinician, dying patient to God.

I was Janet's caregiver during a nine-month experience with adenocarcinoma of unknown primary. From my view (as caregiver), her dying in the church, while working full-time, then part-time, but never not working, was a debacle. A devastation. A secret. An unspeakable thing.

My coauthors share with me the golden thread of Janet's life in wonderfully powerful ways. Dale (my dad) suffered my sister's journey of dying in the church as a parent. Janet's best seminary professor, Fred, agreed to enlarge our circle in hopes of affirming the need for the church to speak more openly about dying.

Knowing of other pastors who died while still in ministry, we wondered if it was common for the church to be ambiguous and to avoid talking about dying, even when it was happening to a key individual in their midst. We found a number of respondents who were not hesitant about sharing their recollections and their losses.

In most work situations, death is an event that carries no particular baggage other than the admittedly significant termination of a worker's employment, the absence of that worker from the job, and coworkers' devastation about the suffering and absence of a peer. Few pastors die while serving their churches. Some of those who do, die suddenly. Others die as the result of a longer illness. While every death produces its own network of emotion, the effects on the church of a pastor's often lengthy terminal illness and death can be much more complex and have more subtle and far-reaching results than the impact of a pastor's sudden death. The dying pastor provides an extreme example of the modern church's inadequacy to serve the dying, and if the pastor suffers a bad dying in the midst of the church, who can die well?

As we proceeded into the darkness of the stories our research produced, we recognized the negative critique implicit in the book's opening. Our first acknowledgment goes to those dying pastors whose struggles can challenge us to do better at the end of life. We gratefully acknowledge those informants who willingly shared their memories of the ten churches in which these pastors died.

The support we received from others was terribly important. We must acknowledge and thank those of Janet's congregation who helped her complete her call in the midst of tension, fear, and unknowing. Since the infancy of this work, Katherine Rowe has been supportive and faithful in advising us through its various challenges and celebrations. Dave Schneider fueled our efforts by repeatedly pointing out that church resources for supporting the terminally ill just weren't out there. We are most thankful to our spouses and children who have been part of this long journey in their own influential and unique ways.

We are grateful to Rodney Clapp for seeing the promise in the project and for shepherding it through the acquisition process at Brazos Press. He offered a needed fourth hand in shaping the work, championing its core intent, and providing a platform for its appearance.

The southwest branch of the Amarillo Public Library proved absolutely indispensable as a veritable research library, responding to constant interlibrary loan requests and procuring resources throughout the writing of this manuscript.

Finally, we acknowledge that this is not a story about one death—that incomparable loss of my beloved sister—nor of ten dying pastors, nor of the grief that attends death. Rather, it is about the larger narrative of God's loving care for all creation and Christ's call to the church to carry the dying on life's last journey.

Joy Goldsmith (for Fred Craddock and Dale Goldsmith)
Blairsville, Georgia
Advent 2011

Introduction

The Christian church has always been cognizant of the need to prepare believers to face dying in a manner fitting to their essential nature as creatures of God—as beings already dead, buried, and raised to new life in Christ through baptism, and sustained in that new physical existence by the Eucharist until called by their creator to the life of the resurrection. That commitment to provide for a good dying has taken different forms throughout history, and the appropriate "art of dying well" has always been clearly articulated—until modern times. Today we find that Christians have ceded to others the scenario for dying; the church no longer has much to say or ways to say convincingly those things it wishes to say.

Words of Jesus, words of Scripture, and sacramental words all constituted the coping tradition for the church's first millennium and were available through worship, sacramental rites, and popular piety. Early in the second millennium, with more individualism and the invention of the printing press, a new vehicle of communication found immense popularity: *The Art of Dying* (or *ars moriendi*) was the title of an immensely widespread collection of warnings, encouragements, prayers, and directions for a good dying that could be accessible to all even if the church was unavailable.

As we enter Christianity's third millennium, we believe it is not too bold to hope that this volume continues the church's commitment to be with and supportive of the dying—that it is a modern iteration of Christian theology of dying in the ancient *ars moriendi* tradition. We do not claim novelty; rather, we offer reminders of the gospel resources available to the dying and we draw on contemporary communication insights that can help us reflect on the ways in which we speak the truth and the comfort available in Jesus Christ, the Word of God, the Lord of the Living and the Dying.

The road map of this journey begins with the dramatic stories of ten dying pastors whose end-of-life days were lived out not only "on the job" but also in the grip of terminal illnesses lived in full view of their death-denying congregations. The dyings were fraught with missed opportunities and marked finally by tragic consequences for the church. This tragic bypassing of the gospel promise is not our story; it is but the sad reality that confronts us if we only take the world's word for it. Chapter 2 offers a broader view of American cultural end-of-life communication patterns and the narratives central to our end-of-life choices. An analysis of how the church has capitulated to a secular narrative closes with the question of how any Christian can receive the benefits of the gospel message for the dying when the church outsources care for the dying to secular caregiving.

The next four chapters look in detail at the Christian narrative and how that story—the one in which end of life can have an entirely new and hopeful meaning—is constituted. Chapter 3 lays out a theology of dying based on the nature, life, death, and resurrection of Jesus Christ, Lord of the Living (and the Dying). Chapter 4 retells the Christian's narrative, in which baptism is the entry and Eucharist the sustaining power for a people who are familiar with dying because they have already died in Christ. We are a community of believers who have *already died* and are already in a new life and equipped to face physical dying in a radically new way. Chapter 5 is a christological examination of Jesus as the *Word* of God, which is the basis and the warrant for Christians who may still need help in talking about the taboos of dying and want to live in a community of communication that includes communication about death. Chapter 6 affirms the need for the church to speak publicly about dying as it brings the full gospel message to a death-defying and death-denying world from the pulpit.

After the organized theological and christological efforts to bring a theology of dying to the reader, chapter 7 offers less organized personal testimonies from ten Christians who, in one way or another, offer thoughts on facing dying as Christians. Each story is different, but each individual relies on Jesus Christ as the means to cope constructively with end-of-life certainties.

Finally, chapter 8 offers a scriptural framing of central criteria for good dying that relies on the breadth of Scripture, Christology and theology, and individual examples offered in previous chapters. A brief offering of practical strategies for communicating on end-of-life issues within the church concludes the volume. Neither the criteria for good dying nor the practical strategies for strengthening communication are exhaustive; rather, these are offered as a stimulus to remember the age-old resources for facing the ending of life that Christians have treasured for centuries.

None of this is meant to replace the role of helping provided by medical science or health care; instead, the role of "being there" in the unique way offered by Christ is encouraged and mapped out in ways that we hope are clear and helpful, but not officious. Each chapter concludes with discussion questions that we hope can be useful to the individual reader and to study/discussion groups committed to the church's mission to bring God's grace to all.

1

The Dying Pastor

Everybody Knew, but No One Would Talk about It

Ten years ago, Pastor Janet Forts Goldsmith died of cancer. Janet died while she was the associate pastor of a mid-sized Presbyterian church in the South. She was the daughter and sister of two of the coauthors (Dale and Joy) and the former seminary student of the third coauthor (Fred). For all of us, she was a light extinguished too early. Janet died within nine months of a diagnosis of metastatic cancer. Terminal illness is stressful for any workplace dynamic. But in this case we noticed that Janet's position in the church made her dying even harder. Her congregation was unable to engage the subject of her dying, to communicate openly and well about it. Denial and ambiguity clouded an already difficult situation. Janet's dying in the church was a train wreck. A disaster. An imposition. An unmentionable thing. The church only many years later is recovering its stability.

Very few pastors die while serving their churches. Sudden death comes to some while others die from protracted illness. Complex and burdensome emotions are produced in either scenario. Here we examine the unique problematic of terminal illness and its complex, insidious impacts on the life and health of a congregation. We recognize the unique circumstances of a dying pastor—yet this provides an extreme example of the modern church's inadequacy in serving the dying and their families. If the pastor suffers a bad dying in the midst of the church, who can die well?

Janet's dying underscored the Protestant church's acquiescence to ambiguity and avoidance concerning dying, even when it is happening to a key individual in its midst. To be sure, the church is expert in dealing with *death*. The ritual and practice of the funeral is performed with exactitude, community, and reliability. But the funeral and what else happens after death is not the focus of this book. Our focus here is on the event of dying itself, and how the church often averts its attention while one of its members dies. We want to call attention to this unfortunate tendency. But more important, we want to remind the church that it has abundant resources to face and engage dying. The church can help its members die well. So ultimately our message is one of encouragement and hope.

First, however, we have to face the situation as it stands. We must explore how churches avoid, deny, cover up, and confuse the reality of dying in their midst. In ten cases we studied closely, pastors faced their dying largely in isolation. And if the pastor's dying can occur so far beyond the ken of the gospel's reach, is there hope that the rest of us can find possibilities for a good dying in the fellowship of the church?

Provisions for Avoidance

Why can we not talk honestly and openly about dying, in our churches and in the surrounding world?

The preeminence of medical science and advanced technology, which have led to the eradication of many diseases once considered death sentences, permit us the belief that we have conquered death, that it is no longer the inevitable, natural progression of life. The ability to receive medical treatment and advanced testing has caused illness to become a permanent condition rather than a temporary state. This prolongation of life has shifted the cause of death from infectious to chronic and terminal diseases. As more causes of death result from chronic conditions, people are living in a dying role longer, thus increasing the necessity of communicating more frequently with dying persons.[1]

Many Americans today see technology as an escape from the inevitability of death and believe that technological advances will fix any bodily damage suffered throughout their lives.[2] Moreover, the attempt to control death has resulted in a loss of understanding of the meanings surrounding dying. Austin Babrow and Marifran Mattson conclude that the dying process has thus become, paradoxically, even more agonizing.[3]

Barriers to communicating openly about dying are a result of a lack of open awareness about dying, society's high expectations and emphasis on health restoration and recovery, and the change from community-based religion to individualized religion.[4] Our care of chronic and terminal illness is medicalized; this replaces the care we could receive from other sectors and institutions of society, the church being a dominant one. The trepidation associated with communicating with dying persons who are seen "as living reminders of the unavoidable reality of death" is commonplace for most of us, and can be the common experience of dying even in our own families.[5]

Medicine has largely usurped our involvement in dying. The loss of public rituals and practices surrounding dying (both cultural and religious) has contributed to communication apprehension in these contexts. Daniel Callahan argues that it is these practices that teach us "the comfort of knowing how to behave publicly in the presence of death—what to say, how to compose one's face, to whom to speak and when to speak."[6]

Church members and pastors are not immune to the ideology of impending death denial. The typical funeral sets a low bar for entry into some rewarding afterlife. That afterlife is typically conceived as a continuation of this life. This in itself is astonishing in light of our increasing knowledge of physics and cosmology. Thus the church typically ignores dying, not on theological grounds but because (1) technology postpones it, (2) culture removes it from view, and (3) the focus is diverted elsewhere. Thus the imponderables are rendered manageable by medicine, technology, institutionalization, and the church's simplistic pandering to a softhearted and softheaded universalism that places an easy judgment on each soul as it ushers them to a heaven that is simply earthly life in perpetuity.

In his survey of Western attitudes toward death, Philippe Ariès describes how our views of death have changed from the natural occurrence that takes place in the bedroom (ideally) to the virtual banishment of dying from our minds by outsourcing it so that it is "hushed up" or "furtively pushed out of the world of familiar things." Death in a medical facility signals a shift from dying as a ritual to dying as a "technical phenomenon."[7]

Helpful Communication Concepts

Medicalization and related factors help explain how and why the church has outsourced the management of dying to institutions other than itself. Some concepts in communication theory will also aid us in understanding how the church fails to properly or constructively engage the dying in its midst.

Diagnosis responses among church family members are as varied as the dynamics in any human system. Other than the patient, family is most immediately affected by a terminal diagnosis: their system is altered and will continue to evolve radically as the pressures of suffering intensify. Research performed in the last two decades recognizes the "intimate reciprocity of suffering by patients and families experiencing terminal illness."[8]

For all parties, there is the individual concern of coping with the suffering of self, as well as the interpersonal concern of coping with the suffering of the other.[9] Both a pastor and congregants share the fatiguing duality of living with and dying of an illness.

Caring for the terminally ill can produce profound psychological effects, increase anxiety and depression, cause deterioration in other relationships, and suppress professional roles and involvement in personally fulfilling and healthy activities.[10] We see all of these familial losses in the churches with a dying pastor. In the church context, basic congregational needs continue and members of a church family likely feel the pressure of increased responsibilities or increasing avoidance of responsibilities. In addition, patient suffering can commingle with these shifting roles of responsibility to create feelings of high anxiety, frustration, confusion, anger, and loss in a church community. Congregational conflict can become untenable as a pastor becomes too sick to participate in the decision-making processes of the church. Amid all this tension and confusion, there are three communication approaches that help us explain how churches can fail to share ideas about a pastor (or member) who is terminally ill: mutual pretense, strategic ambiguity, and Communication Privacy Management (CPM) theory.

Mutual Pretense

The ritual drama of mutual pretense is established when medical staff, church, family, friends, and patient agree to behave as though the patient is not dying. To create this context, a complex, mutually achieved but often unspoken coordination is necessary.[11] If one participant in the context is unable to pretend death is not encroaching, the pretense will end. Of course, mutual pretense is eventually unsustainable if a patient is actively dying. The pretense denies family a closer relationship with the dying patient, leaving the patient very much alone in dying and silenced. The most prominent organizational consequence of the mutual pretense context is that it eliminates any possibility that family and friends might psychologically support the patient and one another in the dying process.

Strategic Ambiguity

In 1984, Eric Eisenberg defined strategic ambiguity as an "instance where individuals use ambiguity purposefully to accomplish their goals."[12] Strategic ambiguity allows points of agreement to be found and values to be shared at an abstract level; agreement occurs in general and the grand narrative of the group is preserved. Conflict can be avoided.

Communicators use resources of ambiguity in language because they always have multiple goals in communicating (though sometimes we are not fully conscious of these goals). The classic example is a person wanting to be simultaneously truthful and tactful. Conversations aimed at breaking bad news or talking about the loss of life as we know it are rife with multiple goals, so it is not surprising that pastors, congregants, and church hierarchy are at times strategically ambiguous.

There are two sides to strategic ambiguity. The first is self-protective, political, and even manipulative—power and privilege can be preserved by avoiding conflict that can occur as a result of directness. The second side of strategic ambiguity is inclusive and even transformative—by avoiding clarity, a communicator can make room for multiple interpretations and in so doing engage disparate stakeholders.[13] Though the properties of this communication strategy can serve an organization and its process, we find that this method used purposefully and passively (without training) presents challenges of vagueness, nonspecificity, distraction, and evasion when a church is confronted by a dying leader or member. The essential problem is this: strategic ambiguity allows people to avoid responsibility for the messages created in a culture of death avoidance. Strategic ambiguity can contribute to the patient and her or his immediate community buying into a story of recovery when it is inappropriate, given the diagnosis.

Communication Privacy Management (CPM) Theory

According to Communication Privacy Management (CPM) theory, private information is owned by individuals and this information is maintained by boundaries. The flexibility of the boundaries and the inclusion of certain people are determined by something called *boundary conditions*.[14] Once private information is shared, the new recipient assumes co-ownership of the information. Boundaries are continually managed between individuals. Terminally ill patients and congregants/staff must ultimately manage co-owned information as a means of managing uncertainty. For example, if two members of a congregation learn of a serious advanced disease diagnosis for another church member, they now must manage that information. Will they share the information and report to supportive others that their co-congregant has a terminal illness? Will they share that their co-congregant has received a difficult diagnosis but is doing well and is committed to recovery? Will they share that their co-congregant has received a difficult diagnosis but is hopeful for recovery? Each choice will have a different impact on the people who become co-owners of this private information.

Thus individuals manage personal (e.g., pastor to congregant), shared (e.g., congregant to congregant, or staff to congregant), and organizational boundaries of private information (e.g., congregant to church hierarchy; parties

throughout the entire structure of the church and its governance) through privacy rules that dictate how a boundary
can operate for people. CPM theory helps us consider what
information is actually exchanged about the dying reality
for a person in the church. Originally proposed as a way of
understanding organizational culture, CPM theory is easily
applicable to family and church systems and is useful in determining group culture during terminal illness. In addition
to understanding boundaries, the ideas held within CPM
theory identify the ways in which people go about managing
uncertainty.

What we found in the churches examined in this chapter
is that uncertainty management was primarily achieved by
avoiding an open awareness of dying as well as limiting access
to private information not only to the local church family but
also within larger governing structures.

A Study of Dying Pastors

In order to learn more specifically how churches respond to
the dying in their midst, we elected to study ten churches,
scattered across the southern and midwestern United States,
that had pastors suffer terminal illness while leading their
congregations. We interviewed interim pastors who replaced
the dying (and now dead) pastors, denominational adminis-
trators, church staff members, and congregants from these
churches. We asked questions such as: How long before his or
her death was the pastor's terminal condition made known to
the church? How did the church discuss—or fail to discuss—
the pastor's dying condition? Was the experience of dying
used to enrich the church's ministry in any way? And what
were the impacts of the pastor's dying and eventual death?

Here we include a sampling of the responses we received
to our inquiries about how these churches coped with and
communicated about a dying pastor. These examples are

qualitative, subjective, and not generalizable, but also truly authentic and rigorous in their experienced detail as represented in the voices of our participants. We believe they provide illumination on how the church faces dying and death in our day; often, as we will see, the church does so with a great deal of avoidance, denial, and confusion. What follows are some of the themes we interpreted from the stories collected.

Communicating a Terminal Illness

Perhaps this is the key moment where we go wrong, or where we at least miss some major opportunities, such as failing to communicate clearly that a pastor is in fact dying. For all of the churches we studied, this seemed to be the least dramatic or quietest event we learned about, but one that casts immense shadows onto how these congregations functioned and communicated as their pastors faltered and as diseases progressed.

In one Texas church, a minister of music told us that the senior pastor knew of his terminal illness "probably" nine months to a year (the uncertainty is telling) before he told other staff, the church board, or anyone else in the congregation. Before then, though he was visibly failing, the gravely ill pastor said nothing about his condition. And when the terminal illness was announced, how did church people talk about it? "They didn't very much," was the reply.

In another case, a dying pastor and his family suppressed any recognition of his condition long after its seriousness was apparent to others. "Everybody knew but no one would talk about it," an interviewee told us. "He kept trying various kinds of treatments . . . and he was not in remission. It was ongoing and he was getting worse and worse and worse." But at no point did this pastor discuss his illness or his dying with the congregation.

Each of these two examples offers a different scenario, but they share the themes of ambiguous communication, congregational denial, and suppression—initiated largely by the pastor. This is not unlike a typical American response to a terminal diagnosis. In the majority of the churches we learned about, the fact that the pastor was dying was denied, suppressed, or ignored by the congregants, even upon a public announcement of a life-limiting illness. Few of us have the opportunity to announce our health updates to congregations in public settings; and in those instances in which pastors chose to share the news of their disease from the pulpit, the weight of this news did not transform the practice of the church body or its outreach, or the performative expectations of the pastor. In such cases, immense dissonance ensues. The caretaker of the people needs care. How do these churches deal with the dissonance? Privacy and boundary management (controlling health information and its impact on organizational function) as well as strategic ambiguity find their stronghold in this tension of need.

The Pastor's Workload in the Midst of Dying

We were interested in how pastors and churches, facing the spiraling challenge of functionality attendant to terminal illness, maintained the practice of pastoring. Some participant responses concerning workload were the most painful to face in our analysis. For many of the pastors who were dying, a concerted effort was made to preserve their preaching appearances. For some, this labor was supported or administered by an inner circle privy to the truth of the pastor's physical dwindling, and for others, church staff were needed to achieve this facade. But as we learned, maintaining the face of a (highly) functioning pastor who was—in reality—dying had a variety of costs for churches that opted for this drama of mutual pretense.

In one case, a sick pastor preached from an easy chair because he was too weak to stand. In another case, a gravely ill pastor kept preaching until three months before his death. His final sermon was interrupted by a seizure. "We wound up having to call the paramedics to take him to the hospital from the worship service," said one of our interviewees. In a third case, a pastor continued to preach after cancer affected his mental processes and he often lost his train of thought.

There seemed to be a potpourri of pastoral crises at these churches with nobody really at the wheel of the floundering congregations. Because pastors at many locations were "so loved," nobody would broach conversations about how they could help the pastor and the church. And other churches allowed pastors to work in contexts that had become dangerous and embarrassing for everyone. They slid further into the drama of mutual pretense, thinking, if not actually saying, things like "These illnesses could be overcome" or "We're one battle away from improvement." Without talking about and planning how to care for the pastor, the pastor's family, the work of the church, and the congregation during this time of decline, most of these churches failed in their mission and suffered a variety of compromises (e.g., loss of financial solvency, abuse of church staff personnel).

Dying and Death as a Consideration

Avoiding the reality of terminal illness extended into an absence and exclusion of this reality from the life and work of these churches. Excluding an acknowledgment of a terminal condition, the probability of dying, and the need to minister to the dying constitutes a conscious (or, more kindly said, an unconscious) positioning taken by these churches. Not only are these dying pastors denied the ministry of the church when they all—including the church—need it most, the larger mission and goal of the church to minister to the needs of the world is delivered a blow from which it is almost impossible to recover.

11

In none of the instances we studied did the dying pastor and his or her congregation respond to terminal illness by facing dying head-on. A dying pastor might be thought to model a Christian dying, but that was not too likely when the pastor and those around him or her would not acknowledge the reality of a life ending and a need for transitions.

In one case, a pastor hoped to model what an interviewee called "hitting hard and winning." This interviewee said, "He talked about his disease but ultimately and evidently privately—always in terms of 'this is how I'm going to beat this thing.'" This posture left the pastor with nothing to "model" once his dying was clear and undeniable.

In another case, the pastor and church colluded to conceal the pastor's impending death by also failing to acknowledge it. In healthier days, the pastor had been a runner and bicyclist. As a gift of hope, the church presented him with a new bicycle. Their intentions were to encourage and support the pastor, but the failure to engage the reality of his dying only encouraged false hopes of his recovery.

The picture was similar in a third case, where, an interviewee said, the pastor was "in total denial." Rather than attempt to in some way discuss even the possibility of his death, church members were "just surviving along with him."

Can a dying pastor find the wherewithal to direct a program about dying to help the church deal with its most difficult reality in leadership? In most of our cases, the answer was no. But also the churches as functioning bodies did not rally to act on their new reality to grow and cope in their crisis, or extend their learning about dying through outreach and mission. What does a dying pastor need? A new racing bike? The mutual pretense of denying death among the pastor's community and the ignorance of Christian tools to aid in this life's transition? We observed that these choices only damaged the churches involved and created wreckage for family and congregations that had lasting effects in excess of a decade at many locations. Table 1 identifies the protracted nature of this experience for several of the churches in our small sample and hints at the costs incurred, which are further described in this chapter.

Impact on the Congregation

Most of these churches lost substantial membership, resources, time, programming, purpose, trajectory, and mission. With the exception of two churches, all the congregations were still continuing to rally and regroup as a result of the experience of the pastor's dying and its management and communication of the illness and dying in and outside of the church body at the time we collected this research. As for Janet's congregation, they are in their tenth year of rebuilding (after two interim and one short-time lead pastor and two associate pastors) and seem to be only now stabilizing and reaching forward with their programming. After conflict and disagreement, the lead pastor announced his departure in conjunction with the session's pledge to allow her to work until she chose to leave or died, whichever came first. With both pastors leaving, the church family was splintered and abandoned.

In the absence of openly acknowledging and planning for a dying pastor's death, another church split into factions after some members thought various other groups were surreptitiously vying to appoint the dying pastor's replacement. Sometimes churches recognized they needed to face a pastor's impending death, but were paralyzed about how to do so. Even as cancer metastasized into one pastor's brain and he became abusive, one church did its best to ignore his behavior. "We were held hostage by his illness," a former staff member said.

Our participants described a variety of hits their congregations incurred, stemming from different causes and traceable to communication surrounding the terminal diagnosis and the role of the pastor in the church. One congregation

Table 1: Summary of Qualitative Data from Sample Churches

Church	Time from Public Acknowledgment of Illness until Death	Summary of Pastor's Work Performance during Dying	Church's Use of Pastor's Terminal Experience to Enhance Church's Ministry	Intervention/help from (higher, outside) Denominational Committees or Officials	Aftermath for Congregation
A	5 years	Worked 6 weeks before death; reduced to sermons only	None	No	Denial of grief; rejection of tradition; schism; did not notify prospective ministerial candidates that former pastor died on the job
B	10 months	Worked until 1 week before death.	None	Yes. Presbytery met with session and urged that associate pastor remain employed as long as associate desired.	Schism; lead pastor left; interim pastor served 2 years; regular pastor served 2 years; another interim pastor served for 2 years before another regular pastor was installed
C	2 years	Worked until death; preaching often incoherently due to illness	Pastor publicly modeled "fight hard and win" vs. illness	No	Much grief; 25% drop in membership, then slow recovery and rebuilding
D	4 years	Worked until 3 months before death; load reduced to sermons only; preached while supported; suffered seizure while preaching	Placed more emphasis on "faith in hard times" in sermons	No	Schism over replacement; leadership instability; 5 pastors have served since death; deceased pastor's wife, traumatized by experience, left community

E	7 years	Although independently wealthy, he worked until 8 months before death; outsourced multiple tasks at cost of $250,000; had fits of anger toward staff	None	Yes; when session realized large outsourcing expenditures, "We were held hostage by his illness for 7 years."	Mutual anger; 3 years of pastoral instability; drop in membership.
F	5 years	Not functional last 6 months but worked until 1 week before death; load reduced to preaching while seated	Series of 3 or 4 sermons concerning "what I have learned as I am dying"	No	Board split over the church's grief process; did not inform applicants for job of former pastor's death
G	2 years	Worked, but with assistant	None	No	"Essentially became 2 congregations" as church split over how to honor deceased pastor
H	1 year	Employed as pastor until death but performed no pastoral function; withdrew to role of congregant	None	No	Initially smooth transition followed by several years of pastoral instability
I	1 year	Worked and resigned 2 months before death	None	No	Recovery and growth
J	6 years	Pastor left church, knowing he could not do ministry full-time; served other smaller parishes part time until a few years before death	None	Yes; after pastor's resignation, church unable to find stable ministry (Intervention was made after pastor's resignation and both before and after his death.)	Interim pastors unable to move church forward; church felt abandoned by the (slowly) dying pastor

in our sample experienced six pastors in as many years in the period following their pastor's dying. Some participants noted the impact of suppressing the dying pastor's story in the church's search for its next pastor, thus leaving applicants unaware of the minefield that awaited the new pastor. This sanitizing of the church's narrative created its own new set of pathologies. As a result, some of these churches failed to grieve and process their experience with a dying pastor for years after it occurred, or they never did so, and new pastors arrived, spending most of their ministry simply identifying the truth of the churches' stories.

One church prepared for its immediate pulpit supply (the Sunday after death) needs, while two others suffered from ill-equipped governance structures. Perhaps these local church governance bodies were overtasked or overloaded, but what can undoubtedly be said for all of the church governance bodies we learned about is that they were not endowed with any practical tools of intervention for churches facing this unique, protracted crisis.

These examples of fracture stem from the same problems: the church (1) communicating poorly about the dying experience, inevitable transitions, and shifting goals; and (2) ignoring its many resources. In some churches, a dying pastor garnered immense power because of his or her diminishing health and the church's fear of discussing dying, and in other churches the pastor lost out in participating productively with the congregation or community because he or she used his or her remaining energy to mediate conflicts, or failed to live up to previously established expectations for preaching performance or organizational management.

Where We Go from Here

In almost all of our ten pastor death stories, the church was either damaged by the experience of dying, or this episode in

16

the church's life brought deep-seated historical problems to the surface. Why is this the case? Employee deaths in other businesses do not seem to have such devastating consequences. What went wrong in the affected churches? Communication Privacy Management theory offers some explanation of the human behavior at play in these settings with the concept of boundaries and understanding the conditions of those boundaries.[15] Often preexisting boundaries established an environment not conducive for productively communicating as a community about a pastor's terminal illness. These boundary conditions, or historical patterns of communication (who gets to know, and how they are told), played substantial roles in each of the churches we explored in this project.

The profoundly hurtful dynamic resonating throughout many of these stories is the same: there was a failure to communicate honestly and substantively within a context provided by the Christian tradition. With the resources available in the church as an institution with a long and rich faith tradition, there ought to be no better place to face death and do the work of dying than within a family of faith. Because of these resources and the promise that rests in this institution, we are hopeful that positive coping resources, through awareness and education about communication, can emerge from the situation we have been describing. The Christian tradition offers a considerable wealth of ideas for communicating about dying. In American culture it is not popular to emphasize dying or to see benefits in it. Nor is there urgency to get the message out before plague, war, nuclear holocaust, or some other blow cuts down the hearers. The fact that most sermons are delivered in front of an American flag suggests that the message is really one of life in the kingdom of America, not death in and toward the kingdom of heaven. Easter, not Good Friday, is the heuristic liturgical paradigm for American Christians. Lively applications of the latest technology make churches look and sound like American pop culture—the culture of the living, not dying.

The organized talk of the church—in Sunday school, discussion groups, newsletters, annual reports, preaching—focuses on the life of the church. But it is a life that unrealistically ignores dying. Dying is not an exciting activity, except in Hollywood. Let us not forget that even the most prominent communication method of all—the multiple individual conversations that church congregants share before, after, and during all events in and of the church—can fail to deal with the substance of the faith and how it addresses dying.[16]

The mystery of dying and death is seldom the topic at funerals; more likely to be the focus is the life of the deceased. It is not how well she died but how well she lived. It is not about the meaning of death, but the incorporation of the deceased—regardless of his or her earthly connection to the church—into a romanticized and trivialized picture of a heaven in which Mr. or Ms. Smith, who did some good things during an earlier life, is now fly fishing or dining with Saint Peter. Unfortunately, the speaker makes use of the bully pulpit to (1) threaten survivors that they had better accept Jesus before they die and go to hell, or (2) to praise the deceased and share humorous anecdotes that are used to "prove" that he or she qualifies for entry into heaven.

What about the dying that led up to death? The time in which (dying) people speak to dying people? Is this a time for the church to employ cultural codes and fight death with surgery, medicine, and cosmetics? The church is much more than a specialized support group established solely for the purpose of giving comfort to one needy but narrowly defined group. It is a generalized support group: the need is living and dying, a problematic for everyone.

The church knows it ought to speak the truth to power. But in the cases of the dying pastors, the calling would seem to be to speak the truth from weakness. This can be a powerful message, particularly if it is not just about "me," the pastor, but about the message of the gospel for everyone. Such truths of the faith can be communicated with a power of been-there-done-that vitality. These are hard stories. They are not remembered for their drama but for what they challenge us to do: regain the church's ministry to the dying, a ministry that has been sidetracked by the church's acquiescence to a powerful secular culture. Telling the stories of these ten churches is a jarring way to start a book on improving the Christian ministry of coping with dying, but the grim realities of failure must be acknowledged in order to see clearly the ways and the means to a better ministry. The inclusion of a communication lens helps sharpen the focus on how the church receives and creates messages to deal with dying in a culture saturated in messages of cure, restoration, and recovery.

It was tragic that these ministers whose dyings have been recounted found so little in the faith resources of Scripture, theology, and Christology that are available to all. And how tragic for the churches in which the dying pastors languished that they were unable to reflect on dying in the light of a faith that illuminated their mission and their shared sufferings. The tragedy was that dying did not "fit" into their Christian story. It is to the rectification of that loss that we turn in the following chapters. While the fact of dying remains, the story into which it can fit more hopefully can change.

In chapter 2 we will broaden our horizon from the ten congregations whose pastors died to the broader perspective of the church's role within an American culture that has medicalized dying and taken it from the church to the clinic. It will be in that wider cultural milieu that the gospel message and the Christian story of dying in faith can unfold and provide a firm foundation on which to face life's final task.

Discussion Questions

    1. Can you see anyone you know (or yourself) in any of the pastors or parishioners described in this chapter?

2. What would be some barriers or pathways to talking about a dying congregant or pastor in your church?
3. How do you see the idea of strategic ambiguity at play in any of the church cases described in this chapter?
4. How are privacy boundaries coordinated in your church? What would you like to change about that, if anything?
5. The drama of mutual pretense requires that all parties play along by pretending that dying is not taking place. How would this drama impact a church's need to transition? What about a church's goals?

2

Victims of the Wrong Story

"Of what story do I find myself a part?"[1] Isn't that a question each of us should also ask? An understanding of our own story, its setting, themes, and trajectory, can help to unravel many of the problems that challenge us. We act out our story and, in turn, the story shapes our thoughts and actions. The stories of the ten pastors' dyings reveal many of the deeply troubling problems faced in dealing with a terminal diagnosis: the intractable nature of disease, the challenge of honest communication among participants in the story, the mercurial course of diagnosis and treatment—from denial to hope to despair to resignation. These are tragic stories in part because of the apparent failure of the churches to offer help from the heart of the Christian gospel at critical end-of-life moments. That failure infected those churches with wide-ranging, deep, and long-lasting effects.

If the church cannot offer hope when someone faces dying, especially when that someone is the pastor, its mission is deeply compromised.[2] We are convinced that the church *can* attend to the needs of the dying and *can* assist the dying to

21

experience a good dying.[3] But this requires an understanding of the reasons why it currently does not and some reminding of the resources at its disposal to do a better job.

When we interviewed participants regarding the dying pastors, we used a number of open-ended questions and did not try to guide the interviews in the direction of specifically religious or Christian answers. As we reflect on the answers given by those who had been involved in the ten churches' struggles with their pastors' dying, we are struck by the fact that absolutely not one word was spoken by any participant that could be construed as carrying any apparently Christian faith connection. These were events that seem to have happened in a spiritual vacuum and were certainly remembered as such. As we step back to take a more comprehensive look at the United States—a "Christian" nation—there seem to be few places where a self-consciously Christian approach to dying can be discovered.

The stories we have told of ten dying pastors need not be accepted as the inevitable way in which individuals and congregations must face the end of life. What was it that could have been different and might have made these dyings less devastating to all concerned? Are there clues in these stories that can show a better way? Is there a Christian way to confront dying and find real help in the face of the inevitability of dying?

A brief diagnosis of what went wrong in the dying of the ten pastors is that the entire approach and handling of illness, care, and final end of life were outsourced. Instead of Christians working together toward a good dying, those involved seemed not to be aware that the Christian faith had anything to offer during that crucial end-of-life "moment," however extended or brief, between diagnosis and death. Instead of seeking the understanding, support, resources, guidance, and strength of the faith of the participant, the public face was denial of death, and trust in science was the private commitment. Just what story is at work here?

Dying Is a Story

We are constantly bombarded by stories that would engage us. The candidate for political office tells the story of his or her vision for the future and invites us in to embrace his platform or give her our vote. The car manufacturer shows us the image of a vehicle that we can believe in. The pharmaceutical company shows scenes of people who have suffered from a certain condition now enjoying life, and we are urged to speak to our doctor about the drug. Hollywood tells us the story of the triumph of right through the strength of a heroic figure, and our hearts tell us that that is the way to a better world. And so on.

We are lured, pressured, bombarded in what one writer called a "tournament of narratives"—each story vying to become *our* story.[4] Story is one way for us to reflect on what we think about life, about the world, our choices, our hopes. Story is both universal—everyone has one (or more)—and uniquely personal. Much of the time our individual and communal stories are probably not at the forefront of our minds. But when serious illness strikes, that illness becomes a part, if not the center, of our story. And the story informed by illness is a story that ought really to connect rather than separate us. With such a story we in some ways become citizens of another place.[5] For the Christian, the issue is one of knowing and cherishing the story of faith in which she plays a role and allowing her personal story to be shaped in such a way that that story about her, whether she is sick or well, can be both uniquely her own and at the same time embraced and enriched by Christ, by Scripture, and by the church.

Death is a condition, a state, but dying is a story. Think of when a friend or loved one died, even if it was in the nanosecond of an auto crash. The dying was embedded in a story full of individual moments, individual events, individual choices, individual actors (some heroes, some villains). There were ups and downs, crises and resolutions, movements from one emotion to another, emotions that raced from euphoria to horror.

Each dying is unique, so statistics and generalizations are inadequate for the one dying and for those who care for the dying.[6] A physician with years of experience with the dying wrote a book in which he gives the general course of illness for a number of the most frequent fatal diseases. But he begins the book with this caution: "Every life is different from any that has gone before it, and so is every death."[7] In describing the increasingly well-known stages and mechanisms of human growth, a physical anthropologist observes that "there is no biological or genetic plan for the aging process . . . because there is no biological reason to age in any particular way. . . . Death is inevitable, but nature did not have the time or the selection pressures to mold our manner of death into a predictable pattern."[8] In other words, even on the molecular, cellular, and organismic level, our dying will be a unique event.

If you were to ask someone who had recently lost a loved one, "What happened?" you would likely get a story rich in detail. You would hear a catalog of symptoms, a diagnosis, perhaps a second diagnosis, the disbelief, the treatment, this medication, that specialist, this procedure, that side effect. The bereaved tells a story. Why? He is trying to make sense of things. He is trying to find out where he now belongs. He is trying to discover if there could have been a different story with a different outcome. He is holding on to the only thing he has left of the person who is no longer there. As one observer puts it, the "stories have to *repair* the damage."[9]

Dying is a story—with events, drama, conflict, crisis, suspense, pain, humor, anguish, sweetness, possibilities, disappointment—that goes on and will continue after someone has died. Dying is not one scene. It is a story unique to the participants and more often than not it is a story that changes everything for us, the actors in it. We are also actors in the stories of others, and when those others enter the final phase

24

of living and begin dying, it is not only their stories that are reshaped by new facts and interpretation; our stories, to the extent that they are intertwined with the stories of the dying, irrevocably change also.

Of course, we do not write our own stories out of thin air. We write them within the framework of larger stories, those stories into which we are born. They are the stories of family, tribe, nation, culture, philosophy, "ism," religion. They are stories that are already written out for us. If we are Americans, they are (usually) set in the United States, celebrated on July 4, shaped by iconic events, and knit together by shared values. Whoever we are and whatever the general outline of our stories, that larger narrative will be rich in texture and in the formative power it has on our own individual stories.

The Christian Story and the Secular Story

Unless that larger story is specifically and explicitly Christian, it will be a story that must be recognized as secular. The root meaning of *secular* is "age" or "eon" or "era." It has come to mean the time over which religion—and we are thinking specifically of the Christian religion and its story—has no dominating role. It is, perhaps, a time between the times of God's rule. Christians pray "Thy kingdom come" because we recognize that we live in a secular ("in-between") period in which God is not accepted as the author of the dominant narrative. We pray for that time to come and our prayer is a manifestation of our own stories: coming together as Christians and identifying ourselves with God's story in a world that rejects or ignores the gospel of God revealed in Jesus Christ. If we simply look at the statistics, we find that our "age" is one in which the Christian story, however it is told, is not powerful enough to grow the church or even maintain its current proportion of the adult American population. That implies that the

Christian story as currently "witnessed" is not compelling in its power, persuasive in its truth, or practical in its usefulness. Other stories are simply more powerful. If this were not the case, the facts and figures about Christian faith and church commitment in the United States would be more optimistic.

The Christian story is not the same as the secular story, despite the fact that many Americans assume a good deal of overlap between "Christian" and "American." Admittedly, there are reasons for the confusion.[10] For example, some think that the Christian faith is a system of propositions to be affirmed, a collection of values to be held, or a list of moral dos and don'ts to be performed. If any of those were true summaries of the gospel, Christian faith and popular opinion would indeed be in agreement. But the Christian gospel is none of those things, at least not first and foremost.

Instead, the gospel in its essence is surely the story of God's goodness, the creation of all that is, the loving and redemptive action of God in the life, death, and resurrection of Jesus Christ, and the promise that finally God will transform all that is into a final and incomprehensibly wonderful new creation.

But this is also, of course, the story of human sin—the free choice of God's creatures to "do their own thing," which allows us to wind up in terrible trouble. It is the story of humans (history) finding and forgetting about the Creator, receiving or rejecting God's chosen messenger Jesus Christ, rejoicing in the creation and in one another, sorrowing, loving, planting, harvesting, warring, marveling, and finally dying and hoping (or not) for a resurrection into a new life promised by the Creator. It is also the story of how we deal with the gifts we are given and with the limitations we confront; how we think about things such as what life is about, who we are, how we are to live, and what meaning the fact of death reveals to us. It is about how we cluster together in families, societies, clubs, gangs, and other associations in order to celebrate life, deal with its challenges, and communicate the meanings about everything that our stories provide us.

The church is where we first hear the language and the plot and find the furniture of our Christian "story"; and that is where we live that story with others. It is where God's story is offered to us and where we intertwine our unique personal story with God's universal and timeless story. The church provides the culture, the environment, the tradition into which Christians are born or "born again," where we learn what it means to be and to live as Christians, where the major rites of passage (birth, adulthood, marriage, death) are celebrated with other people in christenings, weddings, and funerals.

From birth to baptism, through the major events of life, week in and week out, through marriage, to old age (especially old age) and death, the church is the one institution in which people of every age and stage in life should be able to find a place. But even at its best and despite its appropriate claim to be a "one-stop service," the church leaves serious holes in that service and tacitly forfeits its responsibility at critical moments when it seems not to grasp the importance of its common witness at two rites of passage: the transition to adulthood and end-of-life coping.[11]

Unable to Speak of Dying

The story of why we—moderns, Americans, Christians— cannot look at, speak of, or cope with dying is a long story with complex roots and is not the subject of this book. Ours is the story that can provide coping resources for Christians who face a terminal illness. However, the fact is that speaking of dying is something we are unable to do.

Americans are willing to discuss other taboo subjects with aplomb (and even relish). Sex is a good example. "Good sex" has even become sermon fodder in a number of high-profile church programs and sermons. But dying is not a hot topic. It is neither "sexy" nor does it deliver the kind of combat venue and enthusiasm that a good political discussion generates.

Nudity and profanity on TV and in the movies are now almost passé. Death has none of their attractions. Our unwillingness to discuss dying in an open, honest, and sustained fashion is simply assumed to be a part of our cultural and psychological environment.

With the exception of Tolstoy's *The Death of Ivan Ilych*—a masterful depiction of what a dying person feels about himself and his incomprehensible death—it is difficult to think of any account (even fictional!) that attempts to portray dying frankly. Dying is not an appropriate topic unless you use your dying to tell another story. Books like *Tuesdays with Morrie*[12] or *The Last Lecture*[13] communicate about how to live, not how to die.

And yet dying holds an obvious fascination for us. There is no shortage of death in our world to which we are an audience. News cameras are on the spot to record natural and man-made disasters such as floods, hurricanes, famine, and war. Violent death fills our fantasy lives via TV, movies, and comics. Dying titillates us on a 24/7 basis. But why do we not speak about our own or our loved ones' dying?

Our failure to speak honestly of dying goes back a century or so, not very long in our history. This was most originally and famously brought to notice more than fifty years ago by a British anthropologist in "The Pornography of Death."[14] Geoffrey Gorer was prompted by his realization that dying had been increasingly isolated from people, first from children, then from everyone else. He noted some similarities between the ways in which modern people treated sexuality, particularly in pornographic forms, and dying. He noted that just as pornography was a taboo subject, prudishly avoided in public, so too dying was treated as shameful or abhorrent. He noted that the most intense periods of prudery regarding sexuality produced the most pornography. Today, "the natural processes of [physical] corruption and decay have become disgusting" and without a powerful conviction of a future resurrection, "natural death and physical decomposition have become too horrible to contemplate or to discuss."[15] Indeed, "while natural death became more and more smothered in prudery, violent death has played an ever-growing part in the fantasies offered to mass audiences."[16] He concludes with this warning: "If we dislike the modern pornography of death, then we must give back to death—natural death—its parade and publicity, re-admit grief and mourning."[17]

Since the church speaks about dying like everyone else in our culture, why would someone who is dying and asking excruciatingly existential questions want to come into the midst of the congregation that is only accustomed to denying, ignoring, or pretending about death?

In fact, the impetus behind this fear of death is thought by many to have been created by the very science that was prolonging life.[18] The hard sciences supported a new philosophy that could be confident that all reality was physical reality: what you see is what you get. In such a world, the existence of another, heavenly world was improbable. Faith in a future beyond this world had less and less basis. That, in turn, drove us to seek meaning and, more important, success in this life. Failure to find success in this life, as defined by increasingly secular culture, was equivalent to death—a fate to be avoided at all costs. Such costs were mainly in our commitments to affirming the value of whatever secular culture affirmed gave value. We were in a vicious cycle of fearing death, searching for meaning in this life, failing to conquer dying or see hope beyond it, and increasing our commitment to whatever culture promised would save us from death.[19]

The narrative of modern peoples had changed from the story of Christian peoples in earlier times. Despite relative declines in church membership today, most Americans are still associated with a church and the typical church looks quite American.[20] The American flag has pride of place over the Christian flag (nearer the pulpit, higher on the flag pole). The church tends to be priestly rather than prophetic in function; that is, it prefers to carry out the spiritual business of the nation but is hesitant in its prophetic and critical voice on behalf of God in judgment on our failures.[21]

Churches and church members are heavily influenced by American culture and in much of what it does the church mimics that culture. Sometimes the churches' mimicry of American cultural behavior represents an abdication of what could be important expressions of caring faith. Since the "Christian faith requires the shaping of a visible community constituted by material practices that give us ways to go on when we are not sure where we are,"[22] it is important that the material practices that define crucial elements of faith's story be truly Christian when the moment for coping with the end of life arrives.

But that is not what actually happens. Instead, the church is too often absent from "the local geography of dying," where the work of dying is done.[23] The church is not always a factor in addressing the final, if not the hardest, thing people must do. Why? To be blunt, the church has outsourced the work of dying to a secular culture. More precisely, the church has allowed contemporary American culture to rewrite crucial parts of God's great story to suit popular American tastes. The results are devastating.

When confronted with the possibility of dying, even Christians may find difficulty fitting that possibility into an Americanized version of the Christian story. The story offered in American culture is one that has little room for dying—at least for *my* dying. Dying is failure; death is the final enemy.[24] It is a story in which death has not been considered an option and in which one is encouraged to pursue a particular strategy that rejects dying and seeks life at virtually any cost. That is, we just won't talk about it.

So what have we done? We have outsourced the whole business of dying. *Outsourcing* has been a bad word for Americans ever since we realized that it meant that something good (jobs) was being given (by employers) to someone else (not Americans) with bad results (unemployment for

Americans). Outsourcing of the care of the terminally ill is precisely what has happened in the church. Rather than an outsourcing of an economic nature, something far more valuable was outsourced: end-of-life care. Christians were conceding that another community with another narrative about life could provide the primary care for the dying. What was there about that narrative that was attractive or powerful enough to detour Christians in crisis from the gospel?

Who Am I? Secular Identity Theft

There are two main elements to the secular account of things (narrative) that have exerted a powerful attraction to Christians. They are elements of an alien account of things that tempt us in the way our parents were tempted in the garden of Eden, with the appeal that traditional theology has seen in sin: the promise of exceeding our human, creaturely limitations. They are our self-identity and our need to find a silver bullet to aid us in avoiding death.

We allow secular culture to rewrite that part of God's story that tells us who we are. "What are human beings that you are mindful of them . . . that you care for them?" asks the psalmist (Ps. 8:4). According to the Christian's story, we are first and last creatures of God. We were created as social beings who find our fulfillment and our unique individuality not in isolation but in community. The creation story in Genesis pictures not one individual, but two beings (Adam and Eve), each profoundly different from the other and in absolute need of each other in order for each to fulfill his or her own individual potential. Later, Paul gives a different picture with the same point: the church is portrayed as a body, with each member as an indispensable and unique part without which the whole would be incomplete (1 Cor. 12:12–26).

Instead of waiting for God's answer to the "Who am I?" question, Christians have often let the world masquerade as

31

God and tell us who we are. And what alternate story do we confront in our everyday world? Instead of seeing life as a gift that places us in the role of stewards, responsible for the care of what we have been granted, we slip into assumptions about ownership. We think we are our own, when in fact life is a gift. We don't think we will die, so we make no plan for it and are not concerned that the church disregards this final rite of passage and only celebrates the more positive ones. We focus on the now, but a now full of the inconsequential.

Instead of choosing as our road to fulfillment a path that goes through our covenants with one another, we have each individually chosen to go our own way.[25] Such individualism must be understood clearly as sin because it is our choice to define ourselves as independent and attempt to reject God. But it is precisely such individualism that is such a hallmark of American culture. It is difficult for churches to resist and deny such individualism. This "rugged individualism" of American mythology expresses itself in many ways, such as a person saying, "Nobody tells me what to do" or "I make up my own mind." We live in a culture in which we seldom reflect on our contingency—the fact that we are creatures, that we are dependent, and interdependent, and that we will die. Instead, we revel in a youth culture (and the invincibility it implies) and claim an individualism in every arena of life—social, economic, political, and religious.

This individualism is seen in several of the dying pastors of chapter 1, and was the message communicated to their congregations. For example, as we saw, one pastor spoke of how he, on his own, was "going to beat this thing." Other pastors operated independently of the congregation and church leadership to hire additional staff as they weakened but dared not bow out.

For all of us, there is an almost overwhelming temptation to deny our dependency on others. As we approach old age, we resist entering retirement homes and rely on vitamins or plastic surgery, hyperactivity or simple denial to prolong the appearance of youth. When Americans face the prospect of dying, the individualistic response focuses on the maintenance of the individual. Individualism, since it is already an expression of sin, can only express itself in more selfishness, wanting more life, more time, more care, more medication, more from the caregivers. In a material culture *more* is the logical measure of what is of value.

"Our culture seems increasingly moving to the view that aging itself is an illness, and if it is possible, we ought to create and fund research that promises us that we may be able to get out of life alive," notes Stanley Hauerwas.[26] The notorious public meetings reacting to the recent health-care debate revealed an underlying eagerness for each (individual) to have unlimited access to all possible resources of the highest quality of health care, with the implication that no limitations of resources, care, or type of illness should stand between the individual and the battle against dying. Not only is this a narrative about the entitlement felt by each individual to an "eternal life" promised by science and health care in a curious alliance with the state, it is a particular manifestation of sin as selfishness.

Finally, and perversely, there is a general religious ethos that tempts both Christian and non-Christian Americans. There is a notion that each individual can have access to religion, spirituality, piety—call it what one may—that serves the individual in a uniquely personal and instrumental way.[27] This is a personalized application of what has been publicly labeled our "civil religion," which is based on the confidence that God has chosen the United States (and virtually all Americans), that we Americans are fundamentally good folks, and that God will reward us all for our good (as defined by us) behavior. Under this broad and commonly shared umbrella, another personal, private, and individualistic feature focuses on life now and the instrumental power of religion to make the individual feel good. This can be adapted by each individual so that the church has occasionally become a vehicle for an idiosyncratic spirituality that is self-serving. This kind of religion serves individuals by providing a smorgasbord of beliefs, ethics, and visions of the good. All the individual need do is pick a suitable set of pieces that fit one's own comfort zone. One student of American religiosity calls it "moralistic therapeutic deism"[28]—a general and vague belief in a God who approves of our individually selected morality with the result that persons feel good about themselves. For many, religion in the United States is a metaphysical pill, not an embracing and redemptive story.

This is a modern innovation in religion, a do-it-yourself religiosity that one can make up as one goes along. It does not need to share in any larger story, such as the broad epic that Scripture reveals about creation, sin, redemption, and final purpose. Instead, this is a religious buffet from which each can choose what feels good. It makes sense for many Americans since it is personalized, do-it-yourself, success oriented, and free from outside obligations. We do not like to be told what to do. Individualism reigns in general; why not in religion? For the present, one's particular mix of religious elements is not very consequential when it comes to the matter of dying.

But in how many arenas of our lives do we simply make things up as we go along? From plumbing to brain surgery, from having a baby to planning a Caribbean cruise, we tend to rely on experts, and usually pay them good money for their services. But since our culture respects individualism and allows each individual to invent himself or herself, the individual facing death is granted great freedom in selecting an appropriate response. There are, however, very few options available (e.g., fight, battle, deny). A church option is scarcely considered. In fact, what would a "church option" be? When the church fails to advertise and employ its own significant resources for coping with dying and mutely stands by when Christians outsource the answer to a fundamental question about the nature of reality—who am I?—it is committing a grave sin of omission. When we fail to witness clearly and consistently that our nature definitely is not one of fundamental individualism but rather is one of creatureliness, we are closing the door to much of the Christian hope for a good dying.

And yet concern with the spiritual in facing terminal illness is being taken with increasing seriousness even at a time when the Christian faith seems to be losing its ability to face and cope with dying. The overwhelming majority of advanced cancer sufferers claim that religion and spirituality are important to them in adjusting to their precarious situations.[29] The "spiritual" as a dimension of human experience is increasingly being taken seriously by medical professionals as something that must be attended to. However, the word *spiritual* has as many meanings as there are persons asking about those meanings. From Tony Walter's definition of it as "anything that gives meaning to an individual's life"[30] to an emphasis on the personal, internal, and individual (in contrast to the general, common, traditional, formal, and accepted-popular), clarifying the nature of "spiritual" not only still lacks specificity but becomes increasingly difficult.

For many, such elasticity is to be desired, and the increasing importance given to the spiritual can then be addressed in ways that are both flexible and applicable specifically to one individual who need not feel obligated to accept and adhere to a traditional definition or content of spirituality.

Despite definitional difficulties, in recent decades "spirituality" has increased in use and popularity as a category. It has answered needs not satisfied by traditional religion, and many people claim to be "spiritual, but not religious" as they find answers to their questions in spirituality instead of organized and traditional sources.

The word *spiritual* seems most often to refer to the internal and subjective and seems based on an assumption that humans have within themselves reservoirs of strength, wisdom, insight, and hope that can suffice when traditional religious, philosophical, and ethical systems fail to satisfy. (The secular version of this is found in psychological efforts to address dying.) Such a broad definition of spirituality is embraced by the hospice movement (though originally a Christian movement, but now broadened to allow for the patient to develop spiritual resources from any source found useful).

Spirituality is, of course, an important aspect of the Christian faith and ought not to be ignored in any coping strategy for dying Christians. But for the Christian, spirituality is both more defined and at the same time more open-ended than secular spirituality.

In the gospel story, the Holy Spirit, God's Spirit, has a clear identity. In terms of identity, the Spirit is divine, holy, eternal, and partakes in the being and activities of God. Thus we hear of the Spirit's presence and activity in the creation (Gen. 1:2), in the prophets, in the conception of Jesus (Matt. 1:18), in some of Jesus's behavior (Matt. 4:1), and in his continuing presence with the new Christian community (Acts 2:4). So the Holy Spirit is not *my* spirit, or the spirit of our church; it is God's and it does what God directs, not what we might want or feel. That in itself is a decisive identifier that distinguishes the Christian Spirit from any other kind of spirit or spirituality. The prophet Joel foresaw the day when the Spirit of God would be poured out upon (i.e., available to) "all flesh" (everyone) (Joel 2:28). It is Jesus who formally inaugurates the Spirit's coming for the full body of the church; that coming brings the promise of peace to the Christian community (John 20:21–22). The Spirit is God's spirit and we are God's creatures.

The fact that we are created and did not cause ourselves to come into existence imposes dependence and responsibility upon us. We are not here because of ourselves. The uniqueness of our DNA is not something we thought up on the way to causing ourselves to be born. The fact that we are someone else's (God's) also suggests a responsibility. That is another way to say that there are right and wrong ways in which we are to live the lives that have been given us. We are not our own, either in our coming into being, our living out our lives, or in the way in which we are called—yes, often by forces beyond our control—to give them up.

The fact is that we are individuals who are put into a world with other creatures who are also responsible to God. We find that there is little that we can do by ourselves. We cannot acquire food, shelter, education, social satisfaction, or the hope of reproducing without the generous cooperation of others. Indeed, as Christians, much of our individual stories are about the fulfillment experienced when we find that our individual uniqueness is needed by others and that their individual uniqueness is just what we need. We do not live to ourselves. Nor do we die to ourselves (Rom. 14:7–8; 2 Cor. 7:3).

The individualism that has the arrogance to believe it controls its own destiny and that it can change the facts of nature in perpetuating its own life entertains a story that is ultimately false and must disappoint. It is a story that has taken a wrong turn and finds itself on a path that goes nowhere. And yet it is a story that is told with the energy and conviction to hide the shame we feel when confronted with the ultimate failure: dying.[31] And unfortunately, many Christians accept and believe that such a story can be integrated into their Christian narrative. It cannot.

Silver Bullet

Stories are not always consistent. Our own stories are not always consistent; they don't need to be. You may combine a clear understanding of nutrition with an uncontrolled craving for chocolate. You may devour travel brochures but never set foot across the state line. The Christian story itself includes elements, experiences, that don't seem to fit together—things like God creating a good world and then patiently watching us make a mess of it, or like Jesus Christ being both human and divine, or like Jesus Christ dying and rising from the dead. So when we note that Christians who confess faith in God Almighty for salvation *also* turn to medical science for salvation from a medical death sentence, we should not be surprised. In effect, we look to medical science for a silver bullet that will save us from death.

The first question usually asked when confronted with a terminal diagnosis is, what shall we do? Appropriately, the clinician is consulted. The clinician will offer some indication of the treatment possibilities called for by the (terminal) diagnosis. Understandably, this "what-to-do" question is the primary question and draws the most interest and sharpest focus. In a situation of trauma, addressing the most immediate issues is appropriate. The one who can provide direction at that moment is the practitioner of science, not of religion.

Science offers much that is positive. Ours is an age of sophisticated technologies in which science seems to have more credibility than religion. Astonishing discoveries occur on an almost daily basis and new medical applications are constantly reported, often with significant promise for reversing or even eliminating diseases. So when a patient's symptoms point to a terminal diagnosis, rather than submit to the inevitable, the typical American establishes a new and fervent allegiance to whatever good news medicine and modern health care may promise. An additional piece of good news is that most affluent Americans have the resources, through health insurance, to pay for virtually any range of tests, medicines, operations, therapies, and specialists needed to combat their particular illness. The story of science and the availability of its benefits to us all is a story most of us hope will include us.

Accordingly, in our study of the ten dying pastors, we heard repeated reports that the terminally ill pastors "kept trying various kinds of treatment," including bone marrow transplants and other advanced methods.

Medical advances have changed the world and certainly have changed dying. Because of new and improved medical insights, medicines, and health-care procedures, we find ourselves in a good news/bad news situation. The good news is that there are cures and relief not earlier available. The bad news is that while it often takes longer to die, the dying is done without the sweetness that such extension might avail because of the rigor of the treatment. In other words, a commitment to extensive use of medical options may mean longer hospital stays and more time spent recovering from therapies. It also means changes in one's story.

Churches seem comfortable with this arrangement and there seems no conflict when brothers or sisters in Christ trust themselves to a doctor, clinic, or medical procedure. This trust can often mimic a religious commitment in its voracious attention to new information, trust in new people, attendance at scheduled appointments, acquisition of a new language, and practice of a new lifestyle. It is astonishing that religious people in the United States seem to be the ones most enamored of extensive medical support in the last days of life.[32] With such a promising new "gospel" (good news) available, it is not surprising that Americans flock to a promise about which most of us knew virtually nothing prior to our illness. For church members, the "conversion" to the Cleveland Clinic, MD Anderson Cancer Center, or the Mayo Clinic may be more fervent and disciplined than their original commitment to the gospel of God's forgiving, sustaining, and promising love. For Christians in these circumstances, commitment to God is often framed as a hope that God will enable the medical establishment to fix the petitioner's problem. A cynic might wonder just who is being trusted, God or the clinician? The evidence offered to invite such trust consists of a mixture of reports of medical triumphs, survival rate data, suggestions (promises?) from a physician, and anecdotal information from new media, TV, and friends. The faith focused on such promises can enable remarkable commitment and devotion, expenditure and hope. This is all the more astonishing because while faith in God is truly, in the words of Hebrews 11:1, "the assurance of things hoped for, the conviction of things not seen," faith in the biomedical gospel ultimately and absolutely results in death. Nonetheless, this conviction of the "hoped for" can narrow the focus of the participant to one goal (survival) sought from one source (science).

But is there not a wider human vision that demands our attention? Is there not a breadth to life that science can only partially satisfy? There are questions about life and death and beyond. There are issues of tasks not completed and conflicts not resolved. These are matters that fall outside of the competence of science.

But for the present, the church seems content to outsource not only the physical care of the ill person but the entirety of care for the dying to caregivers who in their turn are driven by the desire to achieve physical/scientific success—caregivers who have different goals. The church waits until the patient returns, dead or alive, to its fellowship. We do not suggest, as do the Christian Scientists, that medical care be rejected. Instead, we agree with those Christians like the great twentieth-century theologian Karl Barth, who says that "medical art and science rest . . . on a legitimate use of the possibilities given to man [by God]."[33] But science cannot fully minister to the complexity that comes into play as one faces dying. Putting all the eggs of faith into the medical basket radically narrows the vision and scope of the life to which God calls us.

Again, this is not a condemnation of medical science and the healing arts. We are grateful for them. They absolutely have a central place in the broader vision and mercy that the church can bring to the need. If there is criticism in our words, it is of the church's forgetfulness of its own treasures that can be brought to the ministry to the dying. The allure of the scientific narrative of "progress through chemistry" or the promise of the next breakthrough can only be one chapter in the Christian's whole story.

Americans turn in hope to medical care to save them from dying. Their hope is pinned on what John Swinton calls "glorious medicine." "Such an approach is based on narratives of restitution, and accordingly it places great emphasis on the power of modern health care to overcome illness and suffering and, by implication, death. Glorious medicine assumes that through the appropriate application of reason and technology it will be possible to progress toward the development of a cure for all diseases and the elimination of all suffering."[34]

The story line from "glorious medicine" has been labeled a "restitution narrative" by Arthur Frank. He summarizes it thus: "Yesterday I was healthy, today I'm sick, but tomorrow I'll be healthy again."[35] We assume the norm to be health; illness and dying are definitely a deviation from the norm. The secular faith is that we can overcome any threat.

Unfortunately, the Christian story has been assaulted and occasionally overcome and taken over by this kind of triumphalistic thinking. Over the past seventeen hundred years, Christians more than occasionally have read God's story as one in which God and his children have triumphed over "enemies," with the result that Christians have identified God's gracious blessings as their due and just reward for siding with the God of power. In such a (per)version of the divine narrative, God and Christ (and their people) are viewed as powerful and their power is always expected to be used in order to overcome every enemy.[36]

Rather than see the Christian life as revealed or modeled on the cross of Jesus Christ, so that it can embrace all human experience and suffering, the triumphal view of the Christian life is one of success. One outcome of such a triumphalism is a theology of dying that wants to sound Christian but relies on secular foundations and erects only a facade of faith. It goes something like this: when the (secular) clinicians give you a diagnosis of a terminal illness, refuse to accept it as final; do not give in or give up.

The virtue of persistence in the face of long odds sounds commendable. Indeed, it sounds like the true test of faith—believing in something against the longest of odds and the most intractable of facts. This "faithification" of the "fight" response is the transformation of fight into faith, making it (fighting) a Christian virtue.

The theological problem with such an attitude is that it fails to grasp that Christian faith is a relationship between God and the creation, between human and deity, and the content of faith is all about that relationship. While the Christian faith may well have implications for the way(s) in which we understand nature and human invention and our own selves, faith is not the beginning point for establishing some kind of new reality that does not center in God. Nor is it helpful to see faith as instrumental—as some kind of leverage that the ill person can exert over the threatening illness or even over God. Christian faith is always a gift to us from God and is not something we have ginned up, or a power that we created and exercised, especially for our own benefit.

Or, said another way, when the (secular) diagnostician offers a gloomy diagnosis, our refusal to consider it as a probability while instead placing hope on an alternative outcome—a miracle—may be worth considering. But hoping to the point of insisting that the God who is powerful and able to devote himself to rearranging the created world in order to delay the dying that each of his creatures will experience is to tempt God in a way that may foreclose on other ways in which God could be approached. The fact that death is inevitable is bracketed and God is tempted to play the hand dealt by nature in a way that is not God's but rather the petitioner's.

Theologically speaking, however, this closes the eyes of the one who hopes for his or her desired outcome to the reality of God's creation: all creatures must die. To hope for something different is the temptation to imply that God has made a mistake in this case (and possibly others?), will make an exception, or is being threatened.

Or when the (secular) health-care provider offers the diagnosis of coming death, the Christian may be encouraged to seize instead on the idea that since life is a gift from God, it is too precious to be abandoned, even for a killer disease. To argue (with God) that it is to God's benefit to keep his saints alive is an attempt to force a dangerous logic on the Almighty.[37] Indeed, life is a gift. But such a hope—for the retention of a gift primarily on the terms of the one who has received it—misunderstands the nature of that gift.

The recipient of life fails to acknowledge, theologically, that life is not a gift that lasts forever. It is precious and fragile and its length is not up to the recipient—only its quality is. A terminal diagnosis may call for thanksgiving for what has been given rather than complaint about what cannot be.

Finally, when the (secular) clinician offers the diagnosis of a fatal illness, whatever suffering may be associated with it cannot be used as leverage, either with God or with other people, to get something. The hope here is that one's suffering is redemptive, the suffering of Christ being the main example. Indeed, the "shape" of the Christian life is found in the cross and not in the triumphalism of popular Christianity.

Speaking theologically, however, the problem with seeking leverage through suffering is that the only suffering that Scripture and Jesus experienced as redemptive is the suffering endured for others. The suffering of an illness may be painful and excruciatingly lonely, but from the point of view of faith, it is, in itself, not redemptive. Suffering in one's illness is not a means to overcome that illness.[38]

These efforts to faith-force a miracle (with or without scientific help) are not versions of our Christian story but are actually seductive to the fatally ill Christian and are built on the sand of self-centeredness. The object of our faith must be God; the basis of our faith must be God; our hope is with God, not in particular outcomes; life is a gift that is promised a better fulfillment in death; suffering is not inherently meaningful or positive. We must find a theology of dying

43

elsewhere—not in our own wishes and exertion and not in science and the false theology of popular culture. The church needs a theology of dying that has a solid foundation and that gives clear and believable guidance to the church; that is precisely what the reader will find in the following three chapters.

Stages of Dying

So how do we face this prognosis of dying?

Secular stories encourage a general pattern, and the ten pastors of chapter 1 followed that path. For the most part they failed to locate their own unique and positive story in the larger narrative of the Christian faith. What was the general pattern, the secular pattern, so dysfunctional in the stories of the ten pastors and ten churches? The classic study by Elisabeth Kübler-Ross, *On Death and Dying*, summarizing what she thought to be the typical American responses to death, offered a five-stage process through which persons with a terminal diagnosis moved. Those stages were (1) denial, (2) anger, (3) bargaining, (4) depression, and, finally, (5) acceptance.[39] What did we find in the churches described in chapter 1?

We found denial, most tellingly in the form of silence. Partly because of the promise of modern health care, denial of death is possible, at least for a while. Death can not only be denied but also ignored. Our culture and our churches focus on activity, on living—doing things, going places, keeping busy—all evidences of life. When that is our focus, anyone dying is out of focus, out of our framework of comprehension, a distortion of what ought to be. In this case, the church is simply following the world in limiting its vision to one segment of the population: the still-living who do not think of dying.

We found anger. Our culture can be a complaining, bellicose one. "Don't get mad, get even" reads the bumper sticker.

"Go ahead, make my day," says the tough guy. With all this toughness around, what does one do when threatened by a terminal illness? Fight back, of course. In our study of the ten dying pastors, recall the pastor who declared he was "going to beat this thing," facing death on combative terms.

We found a form of bargaining: "I want to live." That wish contains an implicit bargain. The bargain might be that the patient consents to all medical treatment if only he can survive. Or the bargain might be that, if she is allowed to live, the patient will live her life with more appreciation of each moment. As one interviewee told us, a common assumption involving bargaining is that "ministers don't die. I've heard people say that—'but he's such a good minister that he can't die.'"

Interestingly, we did *not* find depression. Because of the unwritten rule of not communicating honestly about what is transpiring, neither depression, despair, nor doubt emerged, at least publicly, even in the presumably accepting context of the church.

We did find acceptance, in a strange form. The patient who fights valiantly receives a kind of acceptance and admiration for battling, for never giving up, for being courageous. The poet Dylan Thomas captured this most American of sentiments in his famous lines, "Do not go gentle into that good night. . . . / Rage, rage against the dying of the light."[40] Americans don't "go gentle"; American Christians don't "go gentle." A typical obituary for the victim of a long terminal illness is: "After a valiant battle with [whatever the disease] . . ."

Ought the church to expect a terminally ill sister or brother to adopt the popular belligerence often displayed in these circumstances? It is clear that end-of-life language in the secular story is warlike, belligerent, self-centered, and aggressive. Is this how the end of life is to be made acceptable? It is not the language of faith. Faith's language is inclusive, relational, directed to others in love and patience. Is the belligerent antagonism of a secular response the most effective use of the time, energy, and other resources of a terminally ill person when those resources are assuredly in limited supply? Admittedly, in another context, but relevant to this one, Paul exhorts his readers to behave wisely by "making the most of the time" (Col. 4:5b). If fighting means putting all the time, resources, and effort into a biomedical commitment at the expense of other uses of time, resources, and strength, what happens to other, more productive and satisfying avenues? What happens to honest communication, truth, and the needs of others? How is it possible to work out what needs to be worked out in terms of existential questions, threatened relationships, that ever-present to-do list, and setting things in order?

The church is the "geography" where good dying can begin and where individual stories of faithful Christians can find deep and nurturing roots in the faith proclaimed in God's story. This is a story liberated from the secular narrative that silences the reality of dying and turns the volume up on a false view of who we are and what can save us.

The Church Needs to Get It Right

As far as we could tell, the ten pastors died in circumstances in which their personal struggles were not soothed by their own faith[41] and were not confined to individual tragedy. In each case there was an impact on individuals in the congregations and on the communal spirit of each congregation both internally and outwardly in program and mission. Finally, there is a reflection in virtually every case of a larger church (represented in what we have called the "hierarchies") that lacked awareness, sensitivity, courage, or knowledge in its inability to intervene in situations that were disintegrating.

In chapter 1, we noted the case of the pastor who continued preaching from an easy chair once he became too weak to stand. In another case a terminally ill pastor was starting to have intermittent seizures. An interviewee reported, "He had a seizure during the middle of his sermon one Sunday morning and two of the men in the church went up and held him up. . . . They stood and propped him up through the remainder of the service."

Church leadership seems to have been paralyzed by the perceived need to care for the dying pastor. As one source said, "When you have major trauma, things happen to people—things happen to congregations." And as we have seen, much damage to the congregations resulted.

The hesitancy to communicate about dying can stretch to unaccountable (and of course dangerous) lengths. After the dying, when it came to searching for a new pastor, two of the churches in our study did not even mention that their previous pastors had died on the job.

When the church outsources the answers to questions of how one shall face dying to a narcissistic, individualistic over-reliance on science that is wasteful of mortally limited resources, the possibilities of sacramental, gracious, covenantal caring and love are compromised, if not derailed. If the diminishing personal resources of the dying one are invested in a self-focused fight, possibilities of mutual ministries are set aside in pursuit of an elusive and doomed goal of survival.

Unfortunately, there is a clear cultural model, and it is the only one generally available to the terminally ill: be strong, don't mention it, don't give in, fight it. This is the default position to which the church has outsourced the facing of impending death. It combines the individualism and toughness of American culture in a manner that focuses all interest and resources on the dying person.

The secular narrative has taken over. We Christians have let that happen. But the secular story doesn't work. It lies about who we are and what will work. The church needs to remember that it has helped Christians die for millennia (see chapters 7 and 8), to reflect on what has been helpful, and finally to understand why it has abandoned its story in favor

47

of another. The remarkable obituary of one of the ten pastors of chapter 1 offers a hint that signals a Christian alternative: "[name] lived with cancer." This represents a monumental paradigm shift that enabled that pastor to direct energy to ministry and faithful living rather than divert it to fighting and surviving. There is a Christian story in which dying can not only be incorporated but can even approach being swallowed up in victory.

Will the Church Face Dying?

The work of dying is a special one that can easily be ignored in the desperate search for answers, for relief, for peace. The church ought not to outsource its opportunities to minister to the dying. It does not need to allow the dying to use their last precious time and strength to pursue elusive goals when the church has the resources to provide for virtually all of the areas critical at this time—moral, spiritual, psychological, and communal.

The good news is that it is never too late to retrofit. The church can change and shake off its dysfunctionality vis-à-vis dying. It can replace the secular culture of denial and fruitless belligerence with one retrofitted with a reformed community identity that takes seriously our baptismal covenant with the Jesus who died and our bond with our brothers and sisters in the faith, with a church that knows, embraces, and retells God's story—a church committed to include each believer's own story in God's greater narrative.

How many churches have had to retrofit themselves architecturally to accommodate those with physical limitations? The church has become aware that those desiring its message and ministry aren't always able to walk up the steps to the sanctuary or down the steps to the fellowship hall. How many have had to retrofit themselves spiritually in order to accept a female pastor?

Here is a new issue: helping the dying with their work, with the most important work they are called to do on their own. Will we retrofit to help us cope with our dying? Help need not, indeed should not, be construed as help to die, as in assisted suicide. The need is the help to live life as fully as possible and as Christianly as possible to the end.

The question is, will the church take the lead and reincorporate care for the dying into its gospel of care? Or will it temporarily abandon them to science until after the total commitment to medical care has achieved death? Such a temporary abandonment can easily be taken as a permanent abandonment by the dying, even though they can "look forward" to having their funeral back in the church.

There are issues of truth telling involved, which in itself has two critical parts: the content (truth) and the delivery (telling). Content and delivery must converge for there to be a genuine Christian coping with the final moments of life.

And there is the need acknowledged by all who deal with the church's ministry to the dying for a theology of dying. While theology may sound like something left to professionals, or seminary professors, or saints, it is actually something that all of us do. Theology is simply the organized and clearly expressed description of our faith. Faith is what we believe; theology spells it out as carefully as possible. While full-blown theology is usually the work of experts, everyone who has any belief can step back from that immediate commitment and attempt a description of it. We might think of theology's relation to faith as similar to the relationship of a recipe to an actual piece of Grandma's apple pie, or that of the US Constitution to an individual American's patriotism.

There is a real need to spell out what Christians believe about dying. Perhaps there is little good theology of dying today because Christians have not incorporated the reality of dying into their faith. The few efforts to construct theologies of dying are in reality theologies of death, which means they focus more on the resurrection and Christian hopes for the

49

afterlife.[42] The following chapters are a biblical-theological attempt to remind the reader (in an organized way) of the resources central to our faith that will be useful in assisting anyone through an end-of-life crisis.

We do not suggest that the church can answer all the needs and questions that the dying might raise. We do suggest that the church can and ought to be the setting in which any issues about dying are raised and in which there is at least a tradition in which many of those issues already have a history and where some answers are proffered.

To the extent that Christians and their communities are unable or unwilling to minister to the dying, we have forfeited a major ministry and in many ways have invalidated other aspects of our message of hope. Are we really ready to abandon the needy at their most desperate, definitive moment? The church's avoidance of dying and its failure to minister more fully to the dying may be one reason for the weakening of the church in today's world. If that is so, we are facing a moment of opportunity for the church to extend the gospel message of hope.

Finally, there is an utterly pragmatic purpose in our writing. Since we live in a culture absolutely committed not to die (OK, to delay death as long as possible), there is an enormous market niche—really a gaping vacuum—for dealing with the reality and complexities of dying. If we can come to understand the challenges of dying, the resources available to understand it and respond constructively to it, and if we can begin to speak honestly about it, we will be doing everyone a service and will be living up to our calling as disciples in a much fuller way.

If the church cannot face dying, cannot live with the dying of its members, the church will be as good as dead for those who are facing death. Most people in the United States will come to a church in the end—for a funeral. Wouldn't it be wonderful if they could arrive a bit earlier? Doing the work of dying better could give the church a handhold to regain its independence from the shackles of a death-denying culture and a dysfunctional life story. The sheer immensity looming before us all in the reality of life's ending poses this question: Will my story be a part of God's story of the redemption promised and revealed in Jesus Christ?

Discussion Questions

1. Think of a member of the congregation who is seriously ill and whose chances for recovery do not seem to you to be good. How is that person thought of and treated by others in the congregation?
2. How often do you hear a sermon that helps you think about dying and what dying might mean?
3. Why is it difficult to know what is the right thing to say to someone who has just suffered the loss of a loved one?
4. What would your response be to a person in your congregation who said, "My doctor says I have an inoperable cancer and don't have long to live"?
5. Tell your personal story. How does dying fit into that narrative? What changes, if any, are you being challenged to make as you share this story?

3

Jesus Christ

LORD OF THE LIVING
AND THE DEAD—AND THE DYING

In what manner can Christians approach dying? Whatever the approach, it should begin with Jesus Christ, end with Jesus Christ, and be thoroughly based on Jesus Christ. And whatever it is, it must be clear enough to understand, write down, and communicate among Christians. Our goal in this chapter is to suggest an organized summary of what Christian thinking (theology) about dying might be.[1] When given a terminal diagnosis, "a person's world-view has been contradicted."[2] So it is important to have clarity about the bases and content of one's Christian faith. This will be easier if the elements of that faith story have been told and retold in the community and incorporated into one's life on a regular basis. The core of that story will be found in Scripture and the core of Scripture is Jesus.

This is not a theology of death; that is a different matter. While there may be overlap between dying and death, a theology of death is, to put it bluntly, about what happens after one dies.

It is about heaven, hell, the destiny of the physical body, and the condition of the soul; it is about judgment and eternity. Not to put too fine a point on it, the theology of death is the speculation of faith, the imagination driven by hope, the aspirations of believers about something that has never yet been experienced by anyone who could return and tell about it. A theology of death is at the same time a theology of resurrection, which again is faith's hope and promise, but an experience not accessible to a precise description. Death and resurrection are God's gifts to us. Dying, on the other hand, involves us much more consciously and is in many ways our own doing.

A theology of dying is about what we experience before death. We already know a great deal about dying—the mechanics, the setting, the psychology, the physiology, the questions. We know a great deal about it but don't always handle it well. The theology of dying should be a summation of facts and beliefs that inspire hope and confidence because they are based on and flow from the life and dying of Jesus Christ who, we believe, came from God to help us in all things.

The construction of a theology of dying will be like Christian theology in general. It will utilize the story of God's care for a wayward humanity expressed most pointedly in the person and work of Jesus Christ. It will utilize the faith that we have in God through Jesus Christ. The theology of dying will basically build itself as we read once again the familiar story of Jesus through the lens of faith. What will make that story helpful in our quest to cope with dying is that we will read it with the specific question in mind: What does Jesus—his words, his life, his dying, and the regard in which he was held by the inspired writers of the New Testament—have to tell us about dying and about how he can provide for our needs at that end-of-life time?

Christians know the story, at least in general. But how well do we know that part of the story that has to do with dying?[3] How well do we know the part of the story that has to do with Jesus's dying? If we as the church are to carry out our ministry to the dying and if we ourselves are to die well, we need solid support and rich resources because this ministry will test us. Such resources can only come from God's love for us. When Christians think about *any* topic, Jesus Christ is where that thinking must start. The story of Jesus is told in the Gospels; summarized in the creeds of the church; assumed and retold and recast in other (New Testament) Scriptures; dramatized in art, music, and poetry. It is a story that has drawn millions to him as God's means to win an erring creation back. It is a classic story. That is to say, it is universal (actually cosmic) in scope, yet it is profoundly and individually human. It is the story of the eternal Son of God *and* the story of Jesus, a person from first-century Palestine. So it is a complex and challenging story. It is compelling because it is a story about dying, that part of his story that put him nearer to us than does any other part of his story simply because of the dying(s) we all must face.

The Christmas bumper sticker "Jesus Is the Reason for the Season" may sound trite, but it is true that Jesus is the reason for the Christian faith. Any practical application of that faith must develop on the basis of Jesus's historical reality and the faith that grew out of his coming into the world, his life, his ministry, his death, and his resurrection. This sounds simple on one level ("Jesus loves me, this I know, for the Bible tells me so").[4] At another level it may sound as though we are inventing something brand new, though this is not true. Instead, it is a matter of remembering what Scripture tells us about Jesus's living and dying and applying it to our living and dying today. The simplest way to find out about Jesus and dying is to start with his story.[5]

Baby Boy: A Real Human Being

Jesus was born. That he was a real human being—physical, material—was from the beginning an important claim about him. In fact, the New Testament begins with the birth of Jesus. While there was a miraculous dimension to his conception, there is early and consistent insistence that he was a human baby with a human mother (Matt. 1:21–2:1; Luke 1:31; 2:7; Gal. 4:4). It is an important enough fact to be included in all of the major confessions used by Christians across the ages. Our celebration of Advent and Christmas makes this as clear as anything in the Christian faith. If Jesus was really and truly born a human, it meant that he was committed to a life that would end in dying. Thus it is the whole of Jesus's life that is, like ours, marked by mortality and dying.

The story of Jesus is that he was "born of a woman" (Gal. 4:4) in a specific place (Bethlehem, manger; Luke 2:4–7) and at a precise time (Luke 2:6). That is pretty much the story for each of us: we each have a mother and were born in a specific place at a specific hour and date. There is a kind of ordinariness about Jesus's arrival that in a curious way makes it special: it makes him just like us. And, of course, since each of us has to die, so Jesus had to die. Again, there is a specificity to it. As each of us will die by a fatal illness, a bullet, a car crash, or of old age, so too Jesus had to die in some particular way.

This is where his story, though still completely human, diverges from our stories. The interesting part is not in the details—in the mechanics of his dying (it is possible that one of us may die as the result of a just or an unjust governmental decision to execute us)—as much as in how he handled his dying. If we had known Jesus during his early years, it would have been impossible to guess how he would die. We might have assumed that he would die pretty much when and how others of his time died. But that assumption would change after Jesus began his public ministry.

He matured in an environment of diversity (Judaism, pagan religions, emperor worship) and toleration (Romans tolerating some peculiarities of Judaism; Jews tolerating Roman overlords). The opposing powers—the political empire of Rome and the religion of Judaism—were delicately balanced to avoid revolt (by the Jews) and suppression (by the Romans). With a typical life expectancy of about twenty-five to twenty-eight years,[6] with half of the newborns dying by age one, and with no hospitals, clinics, life support equipment, insurance coverage, nursing homes, or curative drugs, Jesus would have seen a lot of dying and could have expected to die young.

While Jesus's mortality has embarrassed some, it is in Jesus's humanity that God is able to reach down to actual human beings and enclose us in a loving embrace. So the first piece of our theology of dying is that part of Jesus's story that reveals and insists on his human birth and on his own full and complete humanity, which of necessity includes dying.[7] Jesus, as human, will die. How will that dying connect with our dying? It assures us that *Jesus was human and from the beginning committed to live the human experience; he is like us (or we are like him).*

Messiah: Man on a Mission

Jesus came into public view around the age of thirty when he accepted baptism at the hands of a popular preacher, John the Baptist. Shortly thereafter, the politically and religiously troublesome John was arrested and beheaded at the whim of one of the Rome-appointed kings. By that time, Jesus had set off on his own, gathering disciples to join him in his mission to announce and teach about the kingdom of God and even to heal sick people.

This healing of the sick, associating with social and religious outcasts, and announcing and describing something he called the "kingdom of God" created a stir. That was good news for the needy and hopeless but a threat to the establishment status quo. If we grasp just a few of the features of this new kingdom, we can get an idea of how it was that Jesus was to get into big trouble. For one thing, Jesus did not pay attention to the political, social, or religious divisions that were important to those in power. Nor did he observe the social and religious boundaries that everyone else observed: lepers were never to be touched, yet Jesus touched them; men did not speak to female strangers, yet Jesus had intimate conversations with them; tax collectors were hated, yet Jesus associated with them; people who died stayed dead, yet Jesus raised them to life again.

With that array of attitudes and behaviors, Jesus was a threat to the status quo; he soon was in real trouble. In fact, the trouble started immediately at the outset of his public ministry. And he was in trouble with almost everyone who was in power. (He was not in trouble with people who already had a lot of troubles of their own; they tended to be enthusiastic about Jesus since it seemed that often he was the only one who could or would help them.)

Jesus's supporters began to think (and his opponents feared) that he may have been sent on this mission by God. They expressed this thought by referring to him in a way that revealed that belief: Messiah. Messiah is the Hebrew term that literally meant "anointed [to do God's work]"; it is translated as "Christ" in the original Greek language of the New Testament. Though Jesus never called himself a "messiah," his followers certainly thought that he acted like one. The term "Christ" occurs 531 times in the New Testament. This suggests that the earliest Christians saw Jesus first and foremost as one appointed by God to do God's work in the world.

What this contributes to a theology of dying is the Christians' conviction that whatever Jesus was doing was a part of an assignment from God. If that included dying, it meant that the mission of God's anointed somehow included dying. That mission contributes to a theology of dying because it shows a Jesus who was committed to the well-being of others regardless of the cost.

Prophet: I Must Die

We readers know that Jesus is not only human, but divine. The Gospel writers knew it. They are telling the difficult-to-tell story of a human Jesus who is the Christ on a mission from God and whose dying is part of that mission. We need to try to read the story of Jesus as if we did not yet know the story of the preexistent, divine Christ.

Some considered Jesus a prophet and others did not. Among those who saw Jesus as a prophet were those who observed miracles (Luke 7:16; John 6:14; 9:17), encountered him in conversation (John 4:19), had become followers (Luke 24:19), or simply heard reports about him (John 7:39–40). Among the greetings offered by the crowds that met Jesus as he entered Jerusalem for the final time was, "This is the prophet Jesus from Nazareth in Galilee" (Matt. 21:11).

Even Jesus referred to himself (indirectly) as a prophet (Luke 13:33), but he knew that his role as a prophet would not be accepted by all (Matt. 13:57). There definitely were naysayers, including the Pharisees (John 7:52), and it is not surprising that the authorities, while doubting, took the popular view seriously and planned to do away with him (Matt. 21:46).

For our purposes, the most important "prophecy" Jesus offered was about his own dying. Three times Jesus told his disciples that he must be rejected by the authorities, killed by them, and then rise from the dead (Matt. 16:21; 17:22–23; 20:17–19; Mark 8:31; 9:31; 10:32–34; and Luke 9:22; 18:32–33). Jesus forecast that the authorities were intending to do away with him as a pest who had become a threat to the religious orthodoxy of the Jewish leaders and to the delicate political balance between Jews and the occupying Romans; anyone with any street savvy could have predicted such an outcome.

There is tension and drama in this story. The human actors, from the Roman governor to the Jewish leadership to the disciples to the Jewish villagers and farmers, see a drama working out in which a popular and well-intentioned young man is heading for an inevitably tragic confrontation with the authorities, and they all know that "you can't fight city hall." Jesus will lose. Surely no one took his prophetic tagline about rising after three days seriously.

As we read the story, trying to forget that we know the ultimate outcome, we may be torn and confused, hoping Jesus is correct, but fearing that he is wildly overconfident and naive. His insight into his future destiny did not deter him from pursuing his mission. While dying was on his horizon, he continued the work that God had given him to do.

There is, of course, another level of prophecy: that of speaking for God for the edification, encouragement, and consolation of the community. (See Paul's definition of prophecy in 1 Cor. 14:3.) Viewed in that light, what wisdom, encouragement, or consolation does Jesus offer that relates to dying? Most notably he spoke of the freedom to commit one's life in one way or another. He observed that if we commit to trying to keep our lives, they would be lost. Only in losing one's life to God can one really live. If you keep life, you will lose it; in losing it you find it (Matt. 16:25 par.). There was an implication that we use our life for one thing or for another. There were ways that would be worth it (life) and ways that would not (to lose one's life).

Not long into his public ministry Jesus knew that what he was doing was so upsetting to the Roman and Jewish authorities that they needed to get rid of him. There was an inevitability to the situation that was clear to Jesus. As they recorded this story, the Gospel writers noted the moment when the human Jesus became aware that he was a marked man.

The earthly thread of the story shows clearly how the political and religious leaders were driving events toward a conclusion in which Jesus would be eliminated; surely Jesus could read the signs. Not only did Jesus make clear that his destiny was not just to die, he also anticipated that he would be killed. The evangelists report that. They all—Jesus and his biographers—tell when in his public ministry these signals were given; it was early in his ministry.

Table 2

Gospel	Reader Informed That Jesus Is a Target	Jesus Announces That He Will Be Killed	Disciples' Negative Responses to Jesus's Announcement	Jesus Anointed in Anticipation of His Death	Jesus Dies on the Cross
Matthew	12:14	16:21	16:22	26:6–13	27:32–50
Mark	—	8:31	8:32	14:3–9	15:21–39
Luke	4:29	18:33	—	7:36–50	23:26–46
John	5:18	—	—	12:3	19:18–30

In Matthew, the announcement came in chapter 16; twelve chapters of Jesus's story remain to be told. In Mark, the announcement comes in chapter 8; eight chapters of the story remain. In Luke, the first attempt on Jesus's life occurs in chapter 4, leaving twenty chapters to describe his ministry. And in John, we know that Jesus's enemies are trying to kill him as early as chapter 5 (Jesus tells us he knows in 8:37, 40, and an overt attempt to stone him is reported in 10:31); sixteen chapters of the story remain.

Jesus knew, and we the readers know early on, that he was heading for an early, undeserved death by murder. Jesus knew it early enough that he might have abandoned the course he was on and avoided that death. The death he expected, of course, was death by crucifixion, which was the form of execution that was used by the Roman government. Even if the Jewish authorities wanted him dead, they would need to have the Romans do the dirty work.

Matthew and Mark also tell us that when Jesus announced his impending execution, Peter, the lead apostle, immediately gave a negative response. This was not unlike our habit of denying death's possibility. He told Jesus, "God forbid" (Matt. 16:22) and rebuked him (Mark 8:32) for seeming to accept his fate (or fatal diagnosis). Some time later, Jesus allowed himself to be anointed; it was a sign that he would be dying. (It was common practice to anoint corpses to mask the odor of decaying flesh in a hot, dry climate.)

Jesus's purpose was driven by what Christians believed was his assignment from God: to be anointed, chosen to be God's agent. In other words, to be Christ/Messiah. Two brief incidents, similar to each other, in the larger picture of Jesus as Messiah/Christ portray ways in which those around him responded positively. While his disciples reacted negatively to the prospect of his dying, in these two incidents, two women "anoint" Jesus.

Jesus is anointed with expensive perfume by a woman whose sins Jesus forgave (Luke 7:36–50). This response was seen by Jesus as a loving thank-you for the forgiveness he offered. Anointing is an act that can be seen as either a reflection of God's anointing his Messiah or as preparation for the customary treatment of the body after death, or both. Either way, the dying of Jesus is anticipated in the story and we the readers "get it." Jesus is also anointed by his friend Mary at a dinner party (John 12:1–8). Jesus explicitly says that this is for the day of his burial. These two incidents show that there were some who positively accepted Jesus's dying.

Finally, we note that roughly half of Jesus's public ministry was conducted under the threat of death by murder (or, if you prefer, a legal execution by the Roman government). Jesus was living, working, preaching, teaching, and healing while living with a terminal prognosis. He knew he would die and he knew how he would most likely die.

It is not too much to suggest that Jesus lived much of his life on a kind of terminal trajectory, laboring always with the knowledge that death (murder) was facing him. Jesus's call to live fully as God's creature and servant is fulfilled in the earthly story of the trajectory of Jesus's dying. Another way to see this is to understand that Jesus saw himself as God's instrument, open to God's direction, transparent to God's will; he was not "doing his own thing." This is a story in which the anticipation of dying is not a reason to abandon God's call. Jesus lived by his advice: anyone who would lose his life will gain it. Jesus *undertook his mission from God knowing that it would lead to his dying, and he lived much of this ministry under the threat of dying.*

The Good Shepherd: Caring for Others

What did Jesus think about dying? Did he have any thoughts that would comfort (or disturb) us? What can we know about Jesus's thoughts about dying? Since he did not discourse on the topic, it is risky to speculate on his inner thoughts. But his behavior was reported as public and obvious. For instance, how did he deal with others who were dying, the (about-to-be) bereaved, and the dead? Numerous miracle stories are included in the New Testament in which Jesus is called upon to address the needs of persons dying.

There are four stories in the Gospels in which a person has died or is at the point of death. They are the centurion's servant (Matt. 8:5–13//Luke 7:1–10); Jairus's daughter (Matt. 9:18–26// Mark 5:21–43//Luke 8:40–56); the widow's son at Nain (Luke 7:11–17); and the raising of Lazarus (John 11:1–44).

In two of the stories a dead child is restored to life (Matt. 9:18–26 par.; and Luke 7:11–17); in the third, a servant on the point of death is restored to health (Matt. 8:5–13 par.); and in the fourth, an adult friend of Jesus is raised from the dead (John 11:1–44). What do these miracle stories tell us about Jesus's attitude?

It was amazing that Jesus could raise the dead. But once he had done it, why stop with the small number he did raise? The fact that Jesus brought only four people back to life may seem odd given his ability to raise the dead.

The church believed in Jesus as a kind of shepherd who watched over and took care of the weak. In raising three youths from death (or at least from a deathbed) and from a premature death, he demonstrated care for those who would have been bereaved. In raising Lazarus, perhaps his concern may have been more for the sisters who would find themselves with no means of support than it was for Lazarus himself.

We must infer that all those he saved from death did die later. This suggests that, for Jesus, dying was not the number one problem. Much larger were issues of forgiveness, inclusiveness, and love—all features of the central focus of his preaching of the kingdom of God.

Is it possible—and this is but our guess—that when he began his public ministry, Jesus himself had already "died" to this world? His first words when he burst on the public scene were: "Repent, for the kingdom of heaven has come near" (Matt. 4:17). "Repent," of course, means to change one's mind; Jesus certainly did not share the "mind" of most of those in first-century Judea. He had already "repented." He was already living in God's kingdom and was an advocate of that kingdom. He was physically in Judea, a province of Rome, but he really lived, in his thinking and preaching and dealing with those who welcomed him, in another world. So there is a sense in which Jesus had already died and taken on a new life as a citizen of the kingdom of God.

What can we add to our list of insights that Jesus's story can provide about dying? Jesus used (God's) power to cure and occasionally to raise the dead. Those miracles were neither his main mission nor were they proof of anything beyond themselves. They were what happened in the kingdom of God. Death and dying were not the central concern of the Good Shepherd. Rather, wholeness—the wholeness of the families and households of those unexpectedly dead—was more important than the life of the individual. These miraculous raisings of the dead must ultimately remain mysteries. They do not solve the "problem of dying"; they do not eliminate dying or death. All those whom Jesus helped eventually died (again). What we discover is that Jesus did not shy away from the dying or the dead; he entered into the experience of death and bereavement and (at least temporarily) assuaged the problem. He was the Good Shepherd who was with those who suffered and died. He cared for others. Jesus's care for others was aimed at enabling them to be who and what the creator God had intended them to be. Dying did not seem to be one of the central problems to which Jesus devoted himself. A theology of dying includes the recognition that *dying (or death) is not the main problem that we face as children of God.* Instead, the goal of Jesus's assignment seems to be more focused on *making people into the image of God intended in their creation.*

Lamb of God: Led to the Slaughter

What did Jesus feel about his own dying? We know that he did not want to die when and how he did. That is clear from the story about Jesus's time in the garden of Gethsemane (Matt. 26:36–46; Mark 14:32–43). Accompanied by his disciples, he told them, "I am deeply grieved, even to death; remain here, and stay awake with me" (Matt. 26:38). What a totally human response to an impending death: stay with me.[8] Jesus wanted to be with his friends at this time (even though they kept falling asleep) and he prayed a desperate prayer: "My Father, if it is possible, let this cup pass from me; yet not what I want but what you want" (Matt. 26:39). He prayed this prayer of hopeful desperation no less than three times. Then he left the garden to meet his death. During his execution, Jesus expressed his human needs: "I am thirsty" (John 19:28). He also expressed anguish over his situation: "My God, my God, why have you forsaken me?" (Matt. 27:46). Finally, he "cried again with a loud voice and breathed his last" (Matt. 27:50).

Despite the knowledge of his impending death, and finally even during the crucifixion itself, he continued to carry out his ministry of forgiveness and love. Consider the following: Jesus prayed for his executioners, "Father, forgive them; for they do not know what they are doing" (Luke 23:34). Jesus spoke to the thief crucified at his side, "Truly I tell you, today you will be with me in Paradise" (Luke 23:43). Finally, seeing his loved ones grieving, Jesus spoke, first to his mother, "Woman, here is your son" (John 19:26); and then to "the disciple," "Here is your mother" (John 19:27).

The nonviolent self-sacrifice of Jesus in not resisting the slaughter he experienced at the hands of his executioners stunned those who knew of it. His acceptance of dying removed the ultimacy and enormity of finality from it.[9] It enabled Christians to believe that Jesus had turned the tables on the worldly understanding of death and to see his dying as a powerfully effective action. This aspect of his story is told without any embarrassment. The Christians turned the tables on the Romans, taking their instrument of torment and humiliation and turning it into God's means of rescuing a sinful world. Jesus can do this because the center of his life is not within himself; he lives in and from God.[10]

What can we learn from Jesus's expressions about his own death under the title of Lamb of God? We find that Jesus *really* died and that the death he died was marked by truly human suffering and human concerns. However, Jesus's dying did not keep him from continuing his ministry up until the very end of his life, nor did it embitter him toward anyone else.

Just because Jesus held to the promise of a resurrection does not mean that what he experienced was some sort of "death lite" or that his suffering was not that of any other human dying. What is revealed in the story and in his words is that he experienced the emptiness and abandonment that any human might feel at such a moment of total powerlessness. A theology of dying includes the acknowledgment that *Jesus did not want to die and that when he did die, he suffered a full range of human anguish.* Death no longer was anticipated as the final destruction and cancellation of life because life can be ours as we give it up.[11] And so Jesus was crucified—tempted by friends' desertion, pain, and divine abandonment. But instead of trying to possess more of himself, he commended himself to God.[12]

Bread of Life: For Our Sustenance

Whether it lasted hours or days, crucifixion was not just designed to kill but to kill in an excruciatingly attenuated fashion. Perhaps in anticipation of such a death, the evangelist John reports that Jesus described himself as the "bread of life" (John 6:35). He foresaw that God might be with him in the experience of being crushed in death and that God would restore him in a way that would feed those who had come to him for help. This may be John's anticipation of the coming practice of Eucharist (Communion, Lord's Supper) in which Jesus's body, killed on the cross, would be ritually shared in the church's celebration of his death.

One of the interesting differences among Protestants, Catholics, and Orthodox Christians is the way each tradition depicts the cross: that simple but terrible execution device used by the ancient Roman judicial system.[13] Protestants' crosses are just that: one vertical bar and one horizontal bar. The cross is empty; Jesus is not there. He has been raised from the dead and is seated at the right hand of God (Col. 3:1; Apostles' Creed). Jesus's death is portrayed as a past event and in some ways is "out of sight, out of mind."[14]

In stunning contrast, the cross of Catholics and Orthodox Christians is heavy with the burden of the dying Jesus. In that tradition it isn't a cross; it is a *crucifix*. Every time a Catholic looks at the cross he or she sees Jesus, suffering and dying. He or she sees Jesus performing his work of salvation *in this present moment.* Like the depiction of Jesus in the Letter to the Hebrews, the offering of the perfect sacrifice (Jesus) is occurring in an eternally present moment: right now! This insight of the Catholic and Eastern traditions emphasizes what is an important truth for understanding how Jesus is one who is particularly suited to understand and care for all of those involved in end-of-life situations.

Each cross or crucifix embodies a true part of the story. The Catholic and Orthodox crucifix is correct in calling our attention to the fact that Jesus's death is a reality that persists into our present and is important for our formation as Christians now. The Protestant (empty) cross is correct in reminding us that Christ was not finished by death but that God empowered him to overcome dying and death. Thus it is that the Jesus Christ who really died and who really rose provides Christians with our basic understanding of dying. The cross is a central symbol, so rich it must be empty *and* it must be carrying Jesus; thus we have two true versions, or one complex whole. The cross represents the central saving event in God's searching out and fixing humanity's dilemma. The cross, as means of execution, is a classic example of people killing people—an example of our failure to establish a peaceable kingdom in this world. When this weapon is used to kill God's own Son, God's response is a history-shattering resurrection of Jesus from the death to which men have put him. So "empty" or "full," the cross shows that the dying of Jesus is central to God's work in this world.

It is almost impossible not to get swept up in this story. Scripture reports that Jesus arose from the dead and was seen by his disciples. A short version of much of this thinking is that the dying of Jesus was an atonement (at-one-ment) effected by Jesus between a loving, forgiving God and a self-alienated, sinful humanity. Exactly *how* Jesus's dying made this atonement happen is a mystery we discuss at enormous length and believe without coming to much agreement on the details. We need only add to our gathering notions about Jesus's impact on dying that through his dying Jesus reconciled humans to God. We can leave the explanations to professional theologians. We will pick up that thread in the next chapter because it deals as much with Jesus's impact on believers as it does with the significance of his death for our understanding of dying. It means that Jesus's dying has the possibility of bringing us to a new reality.[15] A full theology of dying must include hints that Jesus gave about himself and his dying. As the Bread of Life, Jesus saw that *his dying could provide strength to future believers*. Surely that applies to any and all times when Christians need strength.

Christology: Nicknames and Accolades

In all of these events, incidents, or topics, Jesus impressed his followers in ways that prompted them to begin to use titles (we might even call them nicknames) in an effort to express their beliefs about what kind of a being Jesus was and how important he was. These were names or titles that captured the essence of what Jesus did in various episodes of his life. For example, as his interest and success in teaching about the kingdom of God became known and popular, it was not a surprise that he became known as "Teacher." As he was perceived as one sent by God, the title "Messiah" (anointed [by God]) became useful. When he could predict his own death and resurrection, "Prophet" seemed appropriate. In his care for others, "Good Shepherd" seemed just right. "Lamb of God" caught the sense of an innocent suffering death as a sacrifice.

These titles became a kind of shorthand for what the earliest Christian believers thought about Jesus. These titles are appropriately called *christological* titles or *Christologies*. There are dozens,[16] of which Lord, Teacher, and Son of God are frequently used examples. The fact that the first Christians used such titles shows how many-faceted and rich the significance of Jesus was.

By familiarizing ourselves and imaginatively contemplating these Christologies, we may be able to find insights into the Scripture's resources on dying. In that way Jesus Christ as Lord of the Living and the Dead (and the Dying), an admittedly cumbersome Christology, will become more meaningful and more user-friendly to us. In addition, as a less personal, yet more organized and useful way, we may also begin to organize the Christian faith's affirmations about dying into a theology of dying.

By this time in our story, however, the weight of the evidence of the Christologies is beginning to reveal something more than mere descriptions of a very special human being. The actions of Jesus and the assessments by his followers are beginning to point toward a supernatural and not just natural being. In fact, John's Gospel culminates with a Christology that is unambiguously supernatural. Christologies are about to move to a new level of profundity and complexity.

My God! God Knows about Dying

"Doubting" Thomas, one of the original twelve disciples, gave Jesus quite an accolade upon encountering him in the upper room a few weeks after the resurrection: "My Lord and my God!" (John 20:28). Perhaps we should not be surprised. To find alive one who had clearly been dead would shake up anyone and prompt some profound rethinking of the ways in which one viewed things.

Jesus Christ knows what we face in dying. The one who calls us to God is not calling from a distant hill or a heavenly perch; he calls as one who has been fully human and who has experienced the full trauma of dying. Against the deniers of Christ's true and full humanity, the early defenders of the faith would proclaim that since Christ took on full humanness in the most total and comprehensive way, humans—any of us—could be redeemed.

What we have in Jesus Christ is a Lord who knows what it is like to die and whose death has benefits for us. He is qualified to speak to us and be with us in our dying. These affirmations give us confidence in Jesus's qualifications to be the Lord of the Living and the Dead (and of the Dying) and to follow him and hear him as we seek to cope in both our own dying and in our ministry to those who are dying.

"My God." This is the "highest" christological title possible: God, full divinity. He is Jesus Christ, Son of God, fully divine. But in viewing Jesus as the fully divine Son of God, there is always the danger that we might fudge on his true and full humanity. This is understandable. It is hard to imagine that a mere human, even a really great one, could have the powers attributed to Jesus. It is a logical impossibility that something or somebody could be both fully human and fully divine at the same time without one aspect compromising or being compromised by the other. This was all sorted out, on paper at least, in the early ecumenical councils of the church.[17] The Christian church resolved these problems by insisting that Jesus was both fully human and fully divine without either aspect affecting or being affected by the other.

Maintaining an orthodox belief at this point is not just an act of intellectual gaming. The complete humanity of Jesus is something that can be abandoned or compromised only at the cost of invalidating his work of salvation in general and his ability to affect our dying in any positive way. Holding that Jesus was fully human and died a totally human death is important for several reasons. First, it affirms God's full commitment to identify with his creatures and come all the way to us in communicating his love. Second, we cannot dismiss Jesus's death as some sort of superhuman or nonhuman stunt, or as a sleight-of-hand illusion. Third, only Jesus's dying as a human can make him truly the Lord of the Living and of the Dead (Rom. 14:9)—*and of the Dying*. In the dying of Jesus, God himself had a complete experience of human dying. Since Jesus Christ was fully human *and* God's son, that puts our deaths in a place where God knows and understands what we experience when we die. Indeed, "the center of the Gospels is the story of dying faithfully"[18]—that is, of Jesus abandoning himself fully to God.[19]

The culminating contribution from the Gospel accounts of Jesus for a theology of dying is certainly this: in the dying of Jesus, God himself has become fully aware of what human dying means. That means that God knows what it means for us to die.

The Rest of the Story: A Christological Theology of Dying

We have concluded our survey of the gospel story of Jesus and come to the realization that this man Jesus, because of his amazing life (and resurrection), was proclaimed as God, Son of God, Messiah (of God). But that is not the whole story. In fact, scholars suggest that the earliest Christians had already come to the conclusion that Jesus was more than simply an impressive human healer/rabbi long before they had all heard, much less read, the written Gospels. Actually, the earliest Christians originally discussed Jesus in a variety of ways, passing the information around by word of mouth. The earliest Christians were Christians because they believed that "Jesus was Lord"; such was the earliest confession of faith. Soon other confessions began to include Jesus's death and resurrection (1 Cor. 15: 3–4; Apostles' Creed).

In our quest to find resources for coping with dying, it is also helpful to know that our Lord Jesus Christ has the keys of death (Rev. 1:18) and by dying gained the experience and power to be acknowledged as the Lord of "both the dead and the living" (Rom. 14:9). This Christology in Romans shows a Jesus Christ at the margins: alive but dying; dead but resurrected. He is thus uniquely qualified to be "Lord of both the Dead and the Living"—and Lord of anyone in between.

Another dimension of Jesus's story is his preexistence. He is the Christ who existed from the beginning with God and through whom the cosmos was made and holds together (Col. 1:16–17). This existence made him able to understand things in a manner beyond our capacity to imagine. He intentionally set aside his divinity, assumed the most humble embodiment of the human condition—that of a servant—and even allowed himself to die the unspeakable death of crucifixion (Phil. 2:7–8). In this way, the divine Christ's experience of being human was inclusive enough that no one is left out. There is no human experience that was not also the experience of the Son of God.

Scripture presents this Jesus Christ to us in various ways— in Gospels, in letters, in a history, and in an apocalyptic vision. Some of these early writings contain the even earlier creeds or confessions of the church. The most concise, cryptic form of communication was that of simple creeds: "Jesus is Lord" or "Jesus died. God raised him from the dead." From such simple, cryptic statements, longer and longer creedal formulations developed. In each, however, the dying of Jesus is a central feature. This "creedal" Jesus—the one who is known more by a title (and the powers that title implies) than by a gospel type of narrative—is one that appears most in the earliest communication formats used by the early church: letters (Paul's; Hebrews; the Catholic Epistles of James, John, and Peter). It is clear from these letters that Jesus's dying was already thought to have profound implications for believers.

In the one historical account in Scripture, the book of Acts, early creedal formulations are frequently quoted as the stories of the disciples' evangelistic work are offered. (Acts 3:15; 5:30; 10:39 are all passages in which Jesus's death is central to the good news of the gospel message.) Jesus's dying and rising are central to the establishment and explanation of his position in God's plan to offer salvation and reconciliation to all of humanity. What does this contribute to a theology of dying? The story of the early church told in Acts insists that Jesus died on the cross; this part of the Christian gospel message was an essential feature of the good news spread by the church and responsible for the attraction that the Christian message held for the many who accepted it. There is no Christian message without the dying of Jesus.

Given that there is no Christian message without the dying of Jesus, what additional christological implications did the early believers find in the Jesus who was held to be divine, preexistent, and now seated in heaven at the very right hand of God Almighty? For that we turn to the rest of the New Testament, first to the Letters and finally to the Apocalypse.

The Dying Christ of the Church's Letters

When we look at the church correspondence collected in the New Testament, we find a community of new believers committed to discovering what it meant to live as Christ-followers in a world that was ignorant of their beliefs and afraid of their practices. Figuring out how to live in such an environment was not easy, and most of the letters of Scripture are either words of criticism or encouragement of their audiences' efforts, or both. These letters come from writers known to us as James, John, Jude, Paul, Peter, and the unnamed author of Hebrews. What contribution to our christological theology of dying do they offer?

The author of 1 Peter clearly states that Jesus's dying has a healing effect on believers (1 Pet. 2:24)—specifically, in taking away sin so that we might die to sin and live to righteousness. The christological titles he uses in this context are those of Shepherd and Guardian (v. 25). This idea is expanded (1 Pet. 3:19) when he shares the narrative about Christ's visit to "the spirits in prison" (Hades? the place of the dead?), implying the expanded redemptive activity reaches backward and forward in time. Jesus's dying connects us with all who have been or will be faithful.

The writer of Hebrews performs some startling transformations as he (re)tells the gospel story. This author relocates the story of Jesus from the dusty byways of Judea to a heavenly, eternal setting. Instead of describing the victimization of Jesus by the collusion of Roman and Jewish authorities in Jerusalem, he places the story in a perfect, eternal sanctuary where Jesus Christ the eternal High Priest offers himself as the eternal once-and-for-all sacrifice that solidifies the salvation of humankind (Heb. 1:3b). "Therefore we must pay greater attention to what we have heard [Heb. 2:1a], . . . Jesus . . . because of the suffering of death . . . might taste death for everyone [Heb. 2:9b] . . . so that through death he might destroy the one who has the power of death, that is, the devil" (Heb. 2:14b).

In the thirteen letters attributed to the apostle Paul we find repeated references to Jesus's dying and the specific benefits that that death makes available to us. Jesus's dying is specifically "for us," specifically to reconcile us since we had been God's enemies (Rom. 5:10; Col. 1:22).

His dying is comparable (metaphorically) to (our) baptism, so the benefits of his dying are appropriated by us as we are baptized "into his death," and through this "attachment" we can enjoy the benefits of his subsequent resurrection (Rom. 6:3–5; Gal. 2:20; Col. 3:3; 1 Thess. 5:10; 2 Tim. 2:11). The same "transferability" is implied in the difficult phrasing of Philippians 3:10–11: "I want to know Christ and the power of his resurrection and the sharing of his sufferings by becoming like him in his death, if somehow I may attain the resurrection from the dead." His dying is a reality that we can experience; it can possess us: we carry the death of Jesus in the body so that his life may be manifest in the body (2 Cor. 4:10).

In Christ, Paul asserts, dying will be destroyed by being swallowed up in victory (1 Cor. 15:54). Christ's death was a death "to sin" (Rom. 6:10); his death was "for our sins" (Rom. 4:25; 1 Cor. 15:3). In his dying, Christ abolished death (2 Tim. 1:10). The purpose of Christ's dying (and rising) was so that "he might be Lord of both the Dead and the Living" (Rom. 14:9).[20]

The book of Revelation is an apocalyptic vision experienced by John.[21] In this writing, it is axiomatic that there is an intimate connection between Jesus's dying (e.g., his "blood") and freedom from the sins experienced by Christians. Not only that, but Jesus is in possession of the "keys of Death and of Hades" (Rev. 1:18); neither Death nor Hades will be able to keep possession of the dead (Rev. 20:13). The contribution to a theology of dying is a positive one: Jesus, who died in faith (as a martyr), is now in control of death—not just that he "fought the good fight" but that he owns death (like having the keys in Hebrews and there being no more sting to death in 1 Corinthians).

These sections of the New Testament, though written by different authors to deal with different problems in different churches at different times, show remarkable agreement on the basic narrative of Jesus's dying and what that means: in his dying, Jesus created a new reality. His dying effected a new relationship between humans and God by eliminating the divisive effect of sin and by overpowering and taking command of death. The benefits he achieved—new life, freedom from sin, freedom from fear of death—were accessible to any and all who accepted him as Lord. "The meaning of Jesus is not the elimination of death, but rather the reconstitution of [our] identity such that death loses its sting."[22]

The Jesus Christ who died now "owns" death and assures us that he is with us; he knows what it means to die; and he, in his own dying, established a basis on which we can have hope. That basis includes the forgiveness of sins—that is, the elimination of all that is problematic in our relationship with the creator and judge, all that threatens the ultimate possibilities of our lives.

This solid foundation in Jesus Christ and Scripture provides us with the building blocks of a theology of dying, an organized way of thinking about Christian resources to cope with dying. The pieces we have noted in his story to this point include the fact that Jesus's mission (as Messiah) put him in what can be called a "terminal trajectory": doing the will of God assured Jesus of a veritable death sentence; neither dying nor death was the main "problem" to be eliminated by or addressed in Jesus's mission; Jesus really died in the most complexly human fashion; because Jesus is simultaneously God, God knows what human death is; the death of Jesus Christ is understood by the Christians who wrote the New Testament as bridging the sin-caused gap between a loving God and a sinful humanity.

As we seek to cope with dying, our best hope is to do it within this kind of a framework where a great treasury of resources lies. Just *how* the blessings Jesus promises are accessible to the dying will be explored in the next chapter. That will give us an alternative to the defaulting and outsourcing to the secular ideas and practices so powerfully and negatively at work in our times. It can ensure that we seek an understanding of a truly faithful grasp of dying from the one who died for (and like, and with) us.

A Christology of the "Lord of the Dying"[23] offers the church a way to think of Jesus Christ in ways that no other Christology offers; it fills a void in the array of ways in which the church proclaims Jesus Christ to the world—and especially to the dying.

Discussion Questions

1. In what way(s) does Jesus seem significant to you? What does that have to do with your dying or the dying of anyone important to you?
2. Would you agree with the claim made by the writer that the last period of Jesus's ministry was carried out while he was aware of his own death or that he was in some sense "terminal"?

3. Does Jesus's death seem to you like the death of any other person or was there something about it that made it significantly different?
4. How has this review of Christologies (titles of Jesus) broadened your understanding of Jesus?

4

The Difference
Jesus's Dying Makes

How does a theology of dying based on Jesus Christ promise to make our dying a good dying? How can *we* receive the benefits of the theology of dying that come from Jesus Christ and look forward to a good dying? Unfortunately, there are no secrets, no shortcuts, no "dying for idiots" techniques or how-to guides available. The blessings of dying found in Christ are gifts from God and we are invited to accept them. So far, it is quite simple. But the promise we are offered is not just the possibility of a good dying. It is a good living *and* a good dying; it is a whole and total openness to God for a whole and total life. It is an entering into the story that God has intended for his creatures all along.[1] That may still sound simple enough. And it is, as long as we can ignore the competing narratives that offer to define us and satisfy us and direct us in other ways. The way to receive the good dying offered in Jesus Christ is to die in him, now and forever. Once we truly die in him, the promise of rising in him becomes the new life for us, a life in which dying is no longer the problem it once was because we are no longer invested in the life that, in sin, we formerly lived to protect and augment.[2]

We can imagine that at many points in his life, Jesus had options about whom to heal, which Pharisees to visit, what parable to tell, whom to call as a disciple. But there was no option at all at the crucial moment. Only by dying could Jesus complete the work of identifying himself fully with us. Only in dying could he move ahead to death, to resurrection. Only in dying could he fully reveal God. He had been the best teacher, the best shepherd, the most perfect lamb. Now he was to achieve a preeminence among those who have died: God would raise him to be the Firstborn of the Dead (Rev. 1:5). This points to Jesus's resurrection. In the theology of dying we saw that just as Jesus was with us in dying, so too he embraces us in his resurrection. That is wonderfully encouraging and we look forward to that outcome.

But our concern is with what is happening now, before we die, and with how we face the unknown and inexplicable but inevitable reality of our physical dying. How is it that Jesus Christ as Firstborn of the Dead (Rev. 1:5) and as Lord of the Living and the Dead (and the Dying) informs our identity as Christians, particularly in our understanding of and coping with dying?

Jesus took control of death, overcame it, emasculated it. After experiencing it, he took the opportunity to visit the dead (1 Pet. 3:19) before he was resurrected. When the whole series of incredible events concluded, Jesus had died, visited the dead, returned to life, and ascended into heaven. This was not a tourist excursion; instead, it placed Jesus in solidarity with the living, the dying, the dead, and those to be raised from the dead. This is the part of the gospel narrative that declares the power that Jesus Christ has over dying and any threats that dying presents. Dying cannot separate us from him or from God (Rom. 8:38–39).

As the Firstborn of the Dead, Jesus is one of a group, one of many; he is not just the "Lone Ranger" of the resurrection. He is installed by God as the head of the church. The metaphor Paul uses for this group is one that expresses the intimate connection among all the members as well as the unique importance of each: the body of Christ. Jesus invites us to become members of that resurrection body, that new reality. The American model for all this has been one of church membership that has spelled out the requirements expected of those who will be considered Christians and who, on that basis, can expect all the blessings and gifts promised by God.

Where does dying fit in?

Our dying fits in because it is a problem we have, even if we won't admit it. We find ourselves in need. "It is neediness that constitutes the character of our relationship to God," says theologian Arthur McGill.[3] And so we look for help.

If there is one thing that signals the work of Jesus, it is his dying. And Jesus's dying points to and encompasses our own dying. Christians signify our association with the church by "dying" in baptism, and if we derive our spiritual sustenance from partaking in the dying of Jesus in the Eucharist, perhaps it would be helpful to review just what it is that we as Christians are—how our story works out—in light of all that dying.

If it is true, as some say, that the cross is the shape of the Christian life,[4] should not dying play a bigger role in the way we think of ourselves than it typically does? The dying of Jesus has two meanings, each of which finds expression in one of the major actions that identify us as Christians. First, death destroys to bring forth in us a new identity (baptism); second, dying is necessary for the bringing forth of life, as a meal, as a festival (Eucharist).[5]

The Church

To make sense of baptism and Eucharist, we first have to understand in more depth the church, into which we are baptized and with which we celebrate the Eucharist.

When Jesus rose from the dead he was in a unique position. God had not only approved him, but had disapproved of those who killed him. His killers and their institutions stood guilty of a grave mistake: murdering the one whom God had chosen. That immediately made Jesus the center of a new reality, a new community, and those who were attracted to it became the church (the *ecclesia*, the "called out" ones).

The church was where the story was kept, told, interpreted, applied, and transmitted. The church was where Christians wrote their reflections on this new relationship and new understanding of things. The church was where Christians wrote to one another in an effort to be mutually supportive in a world that was definitely hostile to their God, their savior, and to themselves. Their new religion was considered antisocial, deviant, and unpatriotic. Theirs was a life that the powers of the world wanted to stamp out. So they were at work daily to understand the new faith better and live their new lives ever more faithfully. The church is where their story was finally embodied in the Scriptures and where those Scriptures were preserved, translated, studied, interpreted, applied, copied, and passed on, finally, to us.

Originally, in the years that immediately followed Jesus's resurrection, it was hard to become a member of the church. It took serious commitment, a lot of preparation, an extended period of study and, often, sacrifice. Inclusion in the body of Christ meant a lifetime commitment within a larger world that was largely hostile to the movement and scorned its reliance on a dying savior.

As we saw in chapter 2, many Americans see themselves simultaneously as Christians and independent agents. The part of the story that assumes our responsibility to actually live out the Christian narrative and somehow be held morally responsible for our lives has fallen by the wayside. While we expect to be welcomed into heaven by God (or Saint Peter), we do not expect to be greeted with anything even remotely resembling Santa Claus's "Have you been a good girl?"

The discussion of judgment, hell, and meeting one's maker is not a part of our contemporary Christian conversation. Other than a requisite for entry into some—certainly not all—church communities, the seriousness of judgment, moral responsibility, ethical commitment, and punishment for dereliction has become a relic of a past era. We mention these issues not to reintroduce them but to question their loss and wonder if the uneasiness about dying expressed by many is a return of such concerns in another guise, such as anxiety, denial, anger, or bargaining.

Jesus's story and a commitment to life in the church have become optional for many people. The words are there, from "Jesus loves me" to a creed and a sermon. But today's version of the Christian narrative often suffers from one of two problems. One problem is that people do not grasp the message that God in Christ is with us in our dying and that we have died to the world as we became God's in faith. Or that narrative is not one that many people feel they really need in order to take part in the church's life. Statistics suggest that a shrinking portion of Americans show a need for what the Christian tradition offers. The really operative narrative that sustains and compels many in church pews may be a narrative that is never fully acknowledged. Rather than the biblical gospel narrative, it is one that is basically political, tribal, social; it could be from anywhere. What we saw in chapter 1 was the mass abandonment of the Christian gospel story as pastors *and* congregations fled to other narratives that they hoped would sustain them. That abandonment was not a frivolous whimsy: someone was dying. They needed a story that would sustain them. They needed a story that had the overwhelming power that could be gained from the fact that *everyone* believed it to be true. They needed the popular story of restitution offered by a culturally explained and scientifically successful medical system.

For other folks, their long-ago initiation into their parents' or grandparents' church will have to do for their religious credentials. For some, a one-off "rebirth" as a born-again Christian seems to have guaranteed the kind of immortality to which they would like to become accustomed. There is an astonishingly shallow acceptance of this kind of affiliation with God, or Jesus, or a church that is focused on the "death benefits" of the faith. It ignores much of the reality of which those hoped-for benefits are an integral part, namely the story and the life of Christians as found in the community formed around the risen Jesus.

One of the authors still recalls the shock he had while conducting a funeral at a small rural church where he was the pastor. He had been serving the church for three or four years and had gotten perhaps too comfortable with the routines, so it was not unusual on the day of a funeral for him to leave his full-time job at a college for the thirty-minute drive to the church and arrive just in time for a brief heads-up from the local funeral director. This particular funeral was for a person with whom he was not acquainted. Again, this was not unusual because the church was the only one in town and served the entire community; funerals for nonmembers were fairly routine. This time, however, there was a shock. As he read the obituary during the service, and having not read it ahead of time, he came to the last paragraph: "Mrs. Smith has been a member of this church for thirty years." She had? That was news to the pastor!

Sometimes it is embarrassing to belong to a church where half of the members are absent from the main activity (worship) on a regular basis, scarcely ever discuss matters of the faith, and don't seem supportive of the church's missions of service and evangelism. The comedian Groucho Marx once commented that he would not wish to belong to any club that would accept him as a member. The church often seems like such a club: anyone can join, and usually on his or her own terms. They can bring any life-giving narrative along as they associate with a church, and the church doesn't always notice or challenge those competing stories.

But the church is where the gospel story is told and where hearing the Christian story and where living the life of faith can happen. Like it or not, no one can hear the gospel or live the life of faith outside of the church. It is there that Christ invites us to let him include us in his dying so that he can include us in his resurrection. How can that happen? It doesn't happen because the church is doing a wonderful job, but it does happen by means of the church. The church is made of people who have heard this story of hope and have allowed Christ to enfold them in his loving, forgiving care. We hear this story in the church and from the church, and we are free to accept Christ's invitation. That involves joining the church, becoming a part of Jesus's story, and finding a home in the church community. It means accepting God's acceptance of us and becoming a part of Christ's body.

As Christians we take the faith commitment to join the church very, very seriously. This joining is not only focused on what it might mean for our last moments of life, and is not like joining a club, enrolling in a class, or becoming a union member. It is about accepting God's invitation in Jesus Christ to be transformed and to receive a new identity and to be rid of the old (sinful, selfish, possessive) person. There is a larger understanding that accepting God's invitation into his kingdom is for the best not only in the next life but also in this one. For any theology of dying, the serious, long-term commitment to Jesus Christ in the midst of others of like faith is a necessary precondition to receiving, experiencing, and expressing the full benefits of the gospel story. If we have practiced the Christian life, when the time of dying approaches, the whole experience of our past is at our disposal as a treasury of coping resources. That past is something on which to rely and from which to draw meanings. The story we live in the church can be the framework within which to experience a terminal illness. Remembering our story is to "re-member" ourselves, to be restored.[6]

Baptism

From the very beginning (Matt. 28:19, where the risen Jesus commissions his disciples), baptism was the event that ushered individuals into the new community, the church, the resurrection body of Christ. From a formal point of view, baptism could have been thought of as a washing. What was washed? Sin was "washed" away, forgiven. But this suggests the change experienced was external, even superficial—a kind of Saturday night bath, to be repeated next Saturday night. But baptism is much more, much deeper, much more invasive. It is a death. In fact, the main thing about baptism is not about the baptizing or the "washing" at all. It is about God's grace in Jesus Christ that is freely conferred on us. Baptism is a "sacramental assimilation to Christ's death."[7] It uses the water and washing as a symbolic message that we, like Jesus, have died; and, like Jesus, we have risen from the baptismal act as new, utterly transformed persons. We have been emptied of all that we were; it is dead. Now Christ is in us and continues to transform us into new creations (Col. 3:10).

When we decide to accept God's gracious gifts in Jesus Christ, we signal our wish by joining the church. For some, that is a self-conscious, mature decision made as an adult. For others it is a decision made on our behalf by adults (usually parents), a decision that we are intended to confirm when we are older and capable. This decision as infant or adult is expressed in the act of baptism. This is a public display, a personal acknowledgment, and an act of God. It happened because the same God who raised Jesus from the dead restored our relationship to our creator and welcomed us into the church, the community committed to witnessing to the kingdom of God. This profound transformation did not happen because of the water, neither how much is used nor when it is applied.

We should not be surprised that different church traditions practice the form of baptism in different ways. Some want it done early in life, right after birth, to make sure that babies are included in the church. Others want prospective members to wait for baptism until they are adults and can make their own decisions. Each form expresses a different aspect of what is involved in membership in Christ's church. Infant baptism emphasizes God's grace and the importance of the church community, since infants are not yet able to respond to God's offer of reconciliation. Adult baptism emphasizes the importance of the new church member's conscious and serious commitment to God in faith.

The rite or practice of baptism is not magic. Baptism is not like being vaccinated for smallpox or polio. That medical inoculation protects us from the dreaded and often fatal diseases forever. Even better, we never have to give the vaccination or the disease a second thought. It is guaranteed protection from a bad thing.

Baptism doesn't work that way. In fact, baptism doesn't "work" at all. It is a sign, a symbol, a personal statement about one's relationship with God. God's offer of Christ is accepted in a public act of our intention to be a new, reborn person, leaving behind what has separated us from God and poisoned our relationships with others in order to live a new life shaped by God's will.

Unlike a vaccination, baptism does entail a "Then what?" that demands some attention. We are committing ourselves to living the new life that we have been given. After Jesus himself was baptized, he devoted the short time remaining to him before dying to the announcing and establishing of the kingdom of God. Our baptism signals our desire to be formed by that kingdom and the life that Jesus modeled, including his dying. The apostle Paul described that baptism as being baptized into Christ's death: "Therefore we have been buried with him by baptism into death" (Rom. 6:4).

Jesus's death is, among other things, a death to the world and the way the world thinks and acts. As Jesus's baptism had publicized his own rejection of those religious, cultural, political, and military worlds, and as his death removed him from the physical world, Jesus's death to this world under-lined his focus on God and the kingdom of God, a whole story illustrated in prophecy and parable, miracles and wise words. This Jesus and his embodiment of the kingdom of God is what is offered us in baptism.

In our baptism we reject all evil and promise to live a new life. So the Christian's baptism is a symbol of our intent to remove ourselves from these ever-present and powerful worlds that tolerate and enshrine evil and to commit our-selves to the new world: the kingdom of God inaugurated by Jesus Christ. We do this because we recognize that we need to die in order for there to be a real change in our fun-damental identities.[8]

When the Christian emerges from the waters of baptism, she or he has died and emerges as a new person. This is a useful way to see the transformed person. It signals that what we were is not acceptable, useful, or desirable. This person is dead to the life lived prior to baptism, dead to the law (Gal. 2:19), dead to "what is earthly" (Col. 3:5), dead to the devil (Heb. 2:14–15), dead to the elementary principles of the age (Col. 2:20), dead to the old self and to the popular culture of every age or epoch.

Rather than refusing to conform to the culture (or any story other than that of God's kingdom), Paul describes re-pentance in a more positive way: "Do not be conformed to this world but be transformed" (Rom. 12:2). There is a new "shape" to the post-baptism life of the Christian: it is the shape of the cross. It defines a life that is lighter, not loaded by possessions (vocation, family, self), and open to receiving and to giving. It is not only an inner transformation, but one that may be expressed outwardly (so others can actually observe it) in "following Jesus." When Jesus called disciples, he called them to abandon occupations, possessions, family relationships, selves, even lives; the dying cuts deep. But we are not dead to everything.

We are reborn into our vocations and family relationships. We are no longer determined by our possessions. We are alive to God and to others. We are not dead to need—our own need for God, or the needs of others for what we can give. This is a new identity to be expressed in every moment of that trajectory, including the dying end of the trajectory. Dying is not so much a test of faith as an opportunity to continue to express and live that faith, an opportunity to make one last faith decision and commitment.

The dying in baptism is symbolic also of a change that both Jesus and Scripture referred to as *repentance*. "Repentance" is a term that literally means to "change [one's] mind" or to "think differently." Since most of us grow up thinking much the way we have been taught by our parents and by the surrounding culture, we all start out thinking locally. The call to repentance is a call to subordinate local, culturally formed ways of looking at life to the gospel story, and to abandon the narrow confines that hold us captive.

The Christian narrative is unique. Briefly stated, it is that God created the universe and all that is in it, including people, and that all that was created was good, really and truly good (Gen. 1:31 points out particularly that we, humans, were created "very good"). God created us with free will: we could accept God and accept our dependence on him and our connection with other humans, or we could formulate a different plan and try to live a different story and create our own plot. Unfortunately, we did the latter. We decided that we knew best—better than God—and we went our own way. Anyone who has read the newspaper, studied history, or seen people in action knows that this decision has not led to success. Christians call this situation sin; humans acting on their own because they are not taking God (the Creator) and others into account. And once we recognize that we sin and that we are sinful in our self-absorption, we soon realize that we can do nothing about it. Sin can be everywhere, even in our dying. We do not escape the possibility of sinning if we seek to take charge of our own end of life. Karl Rahner warns, "We can also say that mortal sin consists in the will to die autonomously, when death's open orientation towards God . . . is not consented to, and by this refusal a man does not give himself up to the disposition of God."[9]

This is how sin works: we can do it but we can't undo it. In desperation, we may look for help. We may hear about Jesus, his teaching, his ministry, and we may seek repentance—that is, decide that we want what he has and hope that God will bless it with the gift of repentance.

The way offered by Jesus in his teaching and ministry of service was a picture (a story) of what it would be like if God truly were acknowledged to be in charge of the world. What Jesus did was to offer the opportunity for a life richer than the one to which people were limited because of health, religious, cultural, or political constraints. Both his teaching and his works ruffled a lot of feathers of those who had not "repented" of their locally, culturally, politically, and religiously formed ways of thinking. We are called to ignore the thinking of the world and to live in the kingdom of God where our thinking is open to others.

In other words, when we give ourselves to Christ (and to his dying) in baptism, we are saying (to God, to ourselves, and to all the world) that we no longer wish to live (or die) under our own direction, but under Christ's. And in particular, we do not wish to take the matter of dying into our own hands because we see dying as an opportunity for us to be completely open to whatever God has intended for us.

The apostle Paul felt the tension of living in two worlds: this present world (for him, the Roman Empire and Jewish culture) and the world of hope, the kingdom of God. He finally spelled it out: our commonwealth is in heaven (Phil. 3:20). Peter wrote of Christians as exiles and aliens (1 Pet. 1:1; 2:11). Even Jesus could refer to himself as a stranger (Matt. 25:35, 43). The early Christians tell us that when Christ becomes our Lord, we die to this world—its values, its goals, its problems, its comforts, its life-shaping stories, and particularly to its way of treating the whole matter of dying. And we die to our stake in the world—our occupation, our possessions, our families, our selves.

Baptism is public and private; it is a statement to one and all of the changes to which one is committing oneself. It is a completely consuming experience that leaves one utterly and forever changed. Repentance is an ongoing practice for Christians in the church's regular worship. At the point in worship where we publicly confess our sin, said Dietrich Bonhoeffer, "the old self dies a painful, humiliating death before the eyes of another Christian. . . . And it is nothing else but our community with Jesus Christ that leads us to the disgraceful dying that comes in confession, so that we may truly share in this cross. . . . We cannot find the cross of Jesus if we are afraid of going to the place where Jesus can be found, to the public death of the sinner. . . . In confession there occurs a *breakthrough to new life.*"[10] We relive our baptism; we have to relive it constantly considering the pressures we are under to abandon our creator and instead to write our own story (like Adam and Eve tried to do). Bonhoeffer gives what could be a summary of our new life through the death of Jesus:

> God wills the conquering of death through the death of Jesus Christ. Only in the cross and resurrection of Jesus Christ has death been drawn into God's power, and it must now serve God's own aims. It is not some fatalistic surrender but rather a living faith in Jesus Christ, who died and rose for us, that is able to cope profoundly with death.
>
> In life with Jesus Christ, death as a general fate approaching us from without is confronted by death from within, one's own death, the free death of daily dying with Jesus Christ. Those who live with Christ die daily to their own will. Christ in us gives us over to death so that he can live within us. Thus our inner dying grows to meet that death from without. Christians receive their own death in this way, and in this way our physical death very truly becomes not the

end but rather the fulfillment of our life with Jesus Christ. Here we enter into community with the One who at his own death was able to say, "It is finished."[11]

According to our theology of dying, the dying we experience in our baptism awakens us to a new life in the practice of confession in the rhythm of church liturgy. We are refurbished in that new life in accord with a new narrative in which the central fact is the presence of the kingdom of God. Karl Rahner observes, "The appropriation of Christ's death, which transforms the character of our own, is one of these basic acts; not however, coming like a single point in time at the end of life, but rather as a process permeating its entire course. As a consequence, it might by [sic] expected that this appropriation of Christ's death should also have its visible sacramental form in the public life of the Church and this throughout our lives."[12]

As Christians, we believe that baptism is the outward sign of our commitment to God's inclusive and forgiving love. What has happened to us as individuals is not some private secret that, while it may make us feel good, has nothing to do with anyone else. That is why baptism is a public event. Therese Lysaught notes, "As long as sacramental practices are seen as individual-centered therapy for the soul, without regard for their practical, material, corporate nature, they will be limited in their ability to do their work."[13] As theologians of dying we understand that in baptism we have signaled that we have already died a death to the world of sin and have identified ourselves with Jesus in his particular dying and all that his dying has opened to us. In our baptism, we have been grafted onto Jesus and his life by means of his dying, and our lives are lives of dying to an old life, of letting go, of accepting disappointment, and of taking leave.[14]

Who are we? We are repentant, dead, baptized—removed from the world that pushed Jesus Christ aside. We have been emptied of one life and given a new one. We are people who have experienced a death, who know that dying is difficult, but who have found that the new life in Christ is better in every way than a life in a world terrified of death.

Communion or Eucharist

The main activity of the church is that it eats as a community, together, as a family. No, this isn't about the vaunted covered-dish carry-in where the world's greatest meals regularly appear. This is about the Eucharist, the meal celebrated and commissioned by Jesus on the night of his betrayal and arrest. This is not a meal to provide us with the calories, vitamins, minerals, and proteins to keep our strength up. This is the meal that embodies and symbolizes who Jesus Christ is, what he does, and who we are as a result. This is a very small meal with boundless significance for the church, for each participant, and for our theology of dying.

After baptism, our ongoing church life is marked by the rhythms of major moments in the church year—Christmas, Good Friday, Easter, Pentecost, and so on. But these alone cannot carry the burden of the formation of our lives into lives modeled on Jesus. Our continuing formation requires much more, so we regularly, weekly, participate in worship activities that have as at least part of their purpose the forming and disciplining of our lives into the thinking and the practices that can truly be considered Christian.

Most especially, we regularly celebrate the meal variously called a sacrament, the Lord's Supper, Eucharist, or Communion. This celebratory meal is rich in meanings: it is a fellowship meal for the church; it is a sacrificial meal where Christ's death is remembered; it is an eschatological (regarding the end of time) meal anticipating the return of Christ. Regardless of which of these or the many other meanings of the meal that are celebrated, at every instance the words of Jesus are repeated: "This is my body that is for you. . . . This cup is . . . my blood" (1 Cor. 11:24–25). Jesus's dying is the foundation of the celebration. His dying is the central fact in the meanings of the meal as experienced by the participants. Our participation in such a ritual does something to us: we learn these very things through our participation in a way that we could not were we not to take part over and over again.[15]

The individualism rampant in the world's self-understanding does not, and indeed cannot, exist in the church. The church is, after all, the body of Christ, all of us mysteriously but truly bound together in him, in and through his dying. That dying is re-presented and underlies every celebration of this meal.

The sacrament effects Jesus's death in us, again and again.[16] The Lord's Supper frames our response to Jesus Christ in a communal fashion rather than in the individualistic manner culturally praised in the secular world. It shapes us into the (collective) body of Christ.[17] In the meal, Jesus hands his Spirit and his life to us and we are expected to receive those gifts so that we can hand them over to others.[18] This is not the meal of a fast-food world but a time-consuming meal in which Christians take part together. The community (church) has from New Testament times been a family in which none of us dies to himself (Rom. 14:7b). It is a family that, as far as Jesus seems to have been concerned, takes precedence over human families (Matt. 12:46–50). The water of baptism formed a more genuine family than the blood and genes inherited from biological parents. "The primary body through which [the sacraments] work is the Body of Christ, the church," as Lysaught puts it.[19] This being the case, the fictive family of the church has a legitimate claim to be the primary caring unit for dying to the extent that it has a richer and more correct understanding of dying. It is in our being sustained by the dying Christ that we are enabled to sustain others in their dying.

As Christians, we believe that this sacred meal is the central, ongoing ritual by means of which we experience God's presence, blessings, and promises. Whenever we celebrate that meal, we are reminded of our new, Christian story, and our partaking of the meal is a participation in that story. In fact, in eating the bread (body) and drinking the cup (blood) we are all joined physically. As theologians of dying, the meal reminds us of the centrality of Jesus's dying and our collective covenant with him in his dying.[20]

The immediate and practical goal of spiritual formation that Christians seek—those virtues of love, faith, hope, hospitality, patience, caring, and so forth—is not sought for personal display. Each is a quality that only makes sense in relationships—love of . . . , faith in . . . , hope in . . . , hospitality toward . . . , patience with . . . , caring for. . . . The clearest and most powerful place to understand that and be positively moved by it is at the cross, in our participation in the church's central meal.

This is another public statement of our individual submission to the formation called for in the Christian narrative. It is a public display of the church's unity in the dying and rising Christ. When taken seriously, this is life changing.

Incidentally, in this community of Christ's body, the individual place and contribution of each is of immense importance because each makes a unique contribution and is valued for what she or he brings to the whole.

Last Things First: Living in the End Times

The end of the world is now! The *eschaton* (Greek for "end") is here!

For Christians, the end (as in "end of the world") has two meanings. The first has to do with that moment when the world as we know it ceases to exist, when the clock stops and there is no tomorrow. That could be the death of an individual or the point after the general resurrection, when there is no more death. These ends lie somewhere in the unknown future and may not create any feeling of urgency on our part.

But not long ago, some Christian pastors preached a gospel in which the end was understood as something like "the critical moment" or "the crisis," like that pivotal moment when the fever either kills the patient or breaks and the patient survives, or when the hero arrives just in time (or doesn't arrive at all). That crisis moment, according to such a view, is always now. In every story of Jesus's encounter with an opponent, a questioner, or a sick person, that critical moment was in play. In fact, in the original Greek language in which the New Testament documents were written, there were two different words used that can be translated as "time." *Chronos* is ordinary time, often used in English terms such as "chronology" or "chronometer." *Kairos* is a special time: the moment of harvest, birth, or crisis. In this way of thinking, the encounter with Jesus is always special (*kairos*), never ordinary (*chronos*). Looking at it this way, now is always a moment of decision and commitment. Our opportunity to repent and die with Christ and begin a new life could be now, this instant, or it could be missed. Would such a moment of crisis pass and be lost, perhaps forever? Such a view of the end has the benefit of not letting anyone put things off.

This leads to a second Christian meaning for "end." "The last things" are also about the end of the world—as in the goal, the purpose, the final culmination for which God created all things. When "the last things"—God's final judgment, eternal life—are seen in that light, the end of the world is already with us, here, now, in the present moment. In this view, God's judgment is seen throughout Scripture as always operative. And Jesus points out in the Fourth Gospel that we have eternal life (John 3:36; 5:24; 6:47; 17:3) and have it abundantly *now*. Therefore we dare not postpone our thinking about the end (as in final moment) of our days, because the end or purpose of our lives can be known and experienced right now.

How do we make living in the present meaningful and embrace something significant *and* take account of and prepare for our end, the wrapping up of a whole life? Jesus the Teacher draws our attention to the crisis (critical moment in time) in so many parables. Calls to discipleship make the moment of decision a decision with eschatological (end times) implications. The call of the rich man to sell all he has, give the proceeds to the poor, and follow Jesus dramatizes the decisive moment, the moment of decision, when everything is on the line and a simultaneously existential (right now) *and* eternal (forever) decision is called for. Perhaps all of Jesus's teaching about the poor is designed to force us to decide if we will ultimately rely on ourselves or give it all up into the care of God. If we can do the latter, we are ready for death and at the same time fully liberated to be of use to others in the life that continues.

Even in the midst of dying we live on the cusp of absolutely the most critical of all moments: the end and purpose. This double significance of the end flavors our faith narrative in a special way. What is significant and important is not played out on a wider stage. Death presents a double challenge: the meaning or purpose of life and the significance of the future. There is a need for a theology of death now.

The implication of this eschatological thinking found at the heart of the Christian faith is that all things are purposeful. This comes through in several familiar passages in Scripture. Paraphrased, they go something like this: whether we live or die, we belong to Christ (Rom. 14:8); and there is nothing—life or death or anything else—that can separate us from God (Rom. 8:38). The randomness of the subatomic reality revealed by modern physics and the meaninglessness assumed by modern philosophy are trumped by this purposefulness of the Christian faith and its implications for the human experience of dying.

Living with an intense seriousness about "now" does not mean joylessness or that all problems are solved. Indeed they are not. But living seriously as a Christian in *this* moment means that we, like Jesus, can cope with the really tough questions about living and dying. These are the existential questions, the excruciatingly hard ones to deal with, much less answer summarily.

The questions that remain about the end of life are many and varied.[21] Though most such questions may have no sure answers because no one has yet come back specifically to answer them, they are important. Jesus did not come back from death to answer mechanical and detailed questions about death and resurrection, or about the location, architecture, or geography of heaven (or hell), or to provide an activities directory for the afterlife. His resurrection and appearances come as an assurance to those hoping that God's love and power persist in the face of death and sin.

We must learn to live with the kinds of questions that the dying ask, despite not being able to answer many of them. On the one hand, many such questions are unanswerable. On the other hand, the church, in its long tradition, has offered answers that may be helpful. No other resource (or authority) has such a treasury of "answers" to questions about dying and death. The dying may find the church's resources, when offered lovingly and carefully within the context of the covenantal fellowship, comforting and even informative. But our task here is neither to catalog questions nor offer answers; that is both theoretically premature and substantively impossible. Instead, we are simply to be a people for whom God has a purpose. God includes us each in the purpose toward which all things move. As theologians of dying, we hold to the belief that even dying has a purpose within the purposefulness of God's love.

We Christians are called by God and given the gifts of faith in God, hope in Christ, and a love for one another. The structures, ministries, and disciplines of the Christian community are gifts of God provided to assist us in our discipline and our growth in the faith. We are promised that we are moving purposefully toward God. One of the steps will be dying. Usually we don't dwell on that or on other possibly depressing matters. But in a faithful theology of dying, we may trust in God that there could be purposefulness in death.[22]

Earthen Vessels, Exiles, Aliens, Sojourners—with Citizenship in Heaven

Just because we are Christians does not mean we will not face difficulties, stumbling blocks, disappointments, losses, and the inevitable moment of physical dying. One description of Christians acknowledges that "it is *their need and not their love* that relates them to God and relates them to their neighbors. They do not cope with their own needs; they do not anguish over how their own needs may be met."[23]

We are not protected from pain or death, decline or decay. Occasionally, and falsely, there have been protests by some Christians that our primary problem lay in the fact that we are made of material that is physical and corrupt. That has always been false; God creates us good—no, *very* good (Gen. 1:31). "The body is the way we have received God's gift of life in this person," Thomas Long writes.[24] We are earthen vessels and being Christians does not change that (2 Cor. 4:7). What is different for those who have died in Christ and risen to a new life is that they have a new reality and a new understanding in which to experience dying in Jesus Christ.

What does all of this make us? At the least, it makes us people, individually and as a community, acquainted with dying. All of the preceding makes us custodians of the story of the dying Jesus, a community that has already experienced a dying to this world, and one that has risen to a new life because we have been grafted onto the new, resurrected life of Jesus. We are witnesses to the Lord of the dead and the living who welcomes those who are dying to rest in him, ask their questions, share their fears, and work out their problems.

We have these gifts to enable us to cope with all of life, including its dying away. We are blessed, but not proud, for there is much we do not know nor will know until each of us has died to this physical life in Christ. Until then, we have these gifts in our frail hands and are graced by God with the opportunities to use them to aid those with whom we are in sacred, covenantal relationship.

What are the implications for dying and death from this aspect of human response to God's redemptive restoration in Jesus Christ? It certainly means that not only in our living but also in our dying we respond to God's repair of the damage we have done to all others and all things through our own sin. It means that we do not think about dying and death as the world does because we have repented and no longer apply popular and cultural patterns to our lives. For most of us, that means that we have a lot of thinking to do in reforming our outlook and behavior in this valley of the shadow of death.

Americans have been subjected to many story lines about dying. In one, there is a smooth transition to and through the "pearly gates" for the soul escaping the body; in another, the villain achieves redemption in one noble last gasp that solves a murder or resolves a plot (e.g., the melodramatic deathbed conversion); still another involves the romantic (suicide) death of the poet; and the currently popular epitome is the valiant and courageous person "rag[ing] against the dying of the light."[25] Christians have a different story. It is centered in trusting in the one who is the firstborn of the dead and who is strong on our behalf as the Lord both of the Dead and of the Living—and of the Dying. If we are serious about our baptism incorporating us into the death and resurrection of Jesus Christ, then our new (Christian) life begins with baptism and initiates a life of death experiences that forms us in ways that prepare us for physical death.

But still, dying, disappointments, pain, and loss are serious and cannot be dismissed by the power of positive thinking. Nor can they be overpowered by even the most disciplined prayers. There are problems that cannot be ignored, dismissed, laughed off, talked out of, or soothed by drugs, food, drink, or diversions. The Christian faith tradition has space and tolerance for complaints and for those who cry out against God when pain is too great, when injustice or senselessness overtakes, or when there is no help.

Life has more than once failed to make sense to God's faithful. The classic examples are Job of the Old Testament and Jesus in the New Testament. Job was the victim of forces that he neither understood nor could overcome. Jesus was the victim of forces that he understood quite well but was not willing to evade. Even as God's anointed suffered injustice on behalf of humanity, Jesus himself experienced the craziness, absurdness, and loneliness of dying. The cross is not only the mechanism of our deliverance (Ign. *Eph*. 9:1),[26] it is also the metaphor of life not making any sense whatsoever. Jesus screamed out to God, "Why have you forsaken me?" "Explain yourself; this doesn't make any sense!" "I am angry at being left defenseless at the hands of gross malfeasance and injustice. This is absolutely senseless!" This is the cry of a person crushed by horrors beyond his ability to understand and respond.

When we find ourselves in this place—angry, alone, mistreated, misunderstood, hopeless—we know that it is all right to complain. Our burden is not added to by thinking God is behind the terror to punish us or that God is nowhere to hear us. We might remember that for at least some of our misery, there are real human actors operating out of motives that are not positive. This is the unanswerable question of evil, the question of why God allows evil—much of which, of course, is caused by those who reject God. But there is still evil, such as the evil we see in disease.

We are not in the position of the person described in the quip on this church sign: "When you get to the end of your rope, tie a knot and hang on." That is not part of the Christian story; ours is not a story of having to do the hard things ourselves. The reality for many is that when they get to the end of their rope, they have to let go. They can't hang on. That is how they got to the end of their rope! Instead, we have the Psalms. There are psalms with which to express happiness and to praise God for his mighty deeds. And there are laments, psalms that express those emotions of pain and frustration and anger—even anger at God.

The laments of Scripture provide a kind of safety net for us when things are really bad. They help us direct our complaints to God. In fact, they invite our complaints. Their existence assures us that complaining vigorously to God is validated by God. This helps us to say what might be perceived as difficult to say, especially to God. But they also help us by reminding us that these are words that have been used by others, similarly afflicted over the course of centuries. God has faithfully been hearing and hoping to hear from those who need him. The use of the laments encourages us to make our own laments, to cry out as we go through the valley of the shadow of dying, knowing that—because of the dying and rising of Jesus—we can have confidence that God awaits us as we make our final passage.

Since we are dead to this world and regularly pray (in the Lord's Prayer) that God's "kingdom come," it might seem as though we have little stake in this world. Scripture paints a broad panorama of God's people who have known (or been expected to know) that, in the words of Paul, their citizenship was in heaven. From the ancient Israelites, who were chosen and blessed so that they could be a blessing to all others (Gen. 12:2), to Jeremiah, who found the will of God in the fall of Jerusalem and in the opportunity to live faithfully in exile in Babylon, to Jesus, who knew himself to be a stranger in this world (Matt. 25:35, 43), to Peter, whose experience with the world's authorities convinced him that Christians would be aliens and exiles because of their faith (1 Pet. 2:11).

Who Are We?

We Christians are created in the image of God, sinners by our own choice, and unable to reconnect with God or other people. We are blessed because God extends the offer of reconciliation by the gift of Jesus Christ, whose living, dying, and resurrection (if we accept that gift) restores us to God and enables us to live a new life in Christ. We signal that acceptance and that commitment by our baptism (dying in Christ to everything but God), by our life in the church sustained by the Eucharist that nourishes us to be a blessing to all in need, and finally by returning to God in death. This is not a life guaranteed to be a picnic. But even failure, disappointment, pain, frustration, injustice, and abandonment do not separate us from God (Rom. 8:38–39). And of course dying does not separate us from God because we know death, we have experienced it in Christ, and have lived with Christ in us as we consciously and confessionally sought to separate ourselves from any (false) life that could threaten our dependence upon God.

So when we come to die, we are still, first and foremost, God's. That is the "secret" to hopes for a good dying: being God's own. We hear God's promise in the words of the hymn: "I will be with thee, thy troubles to bless, / and sanctify to thee thy deepest distress."[27]

Our deepest distresses are those shared, first and foremost, by God. As we were called to die in our baptism, our vocation has always been one of dying to anything that would separate us from God. Dying a physical death will not separate us from God, as Jesus has constantly shown us.

Our vocation is not to pursue our own lives. We have already died. Our vocation is to live out the life we have been given in Christ. That life will include physical death, but that will neither separate us from God nor from others. When others are dying, we are called to live out that dimension of our vocation: "Are any among you sick? They should call

103

for the elders of the church and have them pray over them, anointing them with oil in the name of the Lord. The prayer of faith will save the sick, and the Lord will raise them up; and anyone who has committed sins will be forgiven" (James 5:14–15).[28]

The vocation of the Christian is to attend to a sick sister or brother and to confront the pains of death with all at our disposal; it may save her or him (from dying, this time) or it may not. The important thing is that all together are committed to wholeness and fellowship with God. This anointing of the sick is the work of the church, of the faithful Christian; it cannot be outsourced to a hospital staff. The anointing of the sick points toward the forgiveness that comes only from God. As Christians become a presence to the dying for whom they care, they learn the final lesson: that they too can accept the same care from others and can hope for forgiveness, acceptance, and reconciliation from God. They can remember that they are made in the image of God, the same God who experienced that same dying in Jesus Christ. The gift of God that finally defines us is the "vocation and the grace to die with him [Jesus]."[29] We are called to love, which has been defined as "the expending and dispossessing and undoing of oneself for the nourishment of others"[30] against which dying has no destructive power. "The love to which Jesus calls us is never the removal of need but *the companion of need.*"[31]

What we have reviewed is the baseline, the foundation of the new life in Christ that issues in a lot of good things: good feelings about ourselves; thankfulness for life and the opportunities that surround us; and clarified responsibilities for our world and for other people, and the resources with which to be of service. Living the post-baptismal life given by Christ is not a life of emptiness (because we give everything we have to others), but a life that constantly receives from God because our lives are now open to God's gifts.

As we look to understanding and addressing the problem for which this book is written, we are now ready to attend to the next step: communicating in truth and love about dying. We have a Jesus Christ who knows dying and whose dying has been overcome by God. We have a God who is with us in and through our own dying. We have been given others: loved ones, acquaintances, those for whom Christ died but whom we do not yet know. Our vocation to visit the sick and be with the dying is informed and strengthened by knowing Christ (and by the theology of dying he has revealed) and by knowing ourselves as already having died and now living new lives in him. We can look forward to accepting our vocation—our call to talk, even about dying—helpfully.

Discussion Questions

1. How does being a Christian and a member of a faith community make the way(s) you approach dying and death different?
2. When you think of the metaphors of dying in Christ or death to sin in baptism, how does that affect your thinking about physical dying and death?
3. What is there about dying or about death (they are different) that is the main problem?
4. In chapter 3 we noted the christological titles that the early Christians included in the New Testament writings that were used to describe the many ways in which Jesus became significant for them: Savior, Messiah, King. We also noted some titles that specifically take account of his dying and the significance of that dying: Lamb of God, Bread of Life. We invite you to participate in the following exercise: take one of the titles of Jesus and ask yourself, if Jesus is the Son of God (or the Good Shepherd, or the Word of God), what does that make me? For example, if Jesus is the Word of God, does that make me a Listener? If he is the True Vine, would that make me totally connected

to and dependent upon him for everything I am? If he is a Prophet, would that make me want to hear all he has to say about God? Use the christological titles that can easily lead us to think of Jesus's dying to do this exercise:

> If Jesus is the Lamb of God, that makes me. . . .
> If Jesus is the Bread of Life, that makes me. . . .
> If Jesus is our Passover, that makes me. . . .
> If Jesus is our. . . .

5. With whom do you want to die? Why?

5

What Do You Say to Someone Who Is Dying?

Where and when do we in the church talk about dying? Sadly, as we have seen, almost nowhere and hardly ever. Certainly during a service of baptism or Eucharist we will hear of Jesus's dying. We also hear of his death in the confession and perhaps the occasional "Jesus died for you" in a sermon. But even the latter kind of reference may be a response made more to a scripted and mechanical piece of "God's plan" than to the truly human experience of terror, sadness, pain, injustice, and abandonment that Jesus experienced and that has something concrete and specific to say about *my* dying.

But we do not despair. The reality of Jesus's dying for and with us is our main hope for strength at the end of life. Scripture provides us with insights into the riches of his gift. And we have already died to all that can separate us from God and that threatens to make dying wretchedly destructive.

The Bible Says . . .

Let us begin again with Scripture. It may be surprising for us to learn that the very first problem expressed by the early Christians in Scripture is the question, if any die before Christ returns to take the believers to heaven, what will their fate be in the resurrection? (1 Thess. 4:13–18). It is possible that some of the Thessalonian Christians who were asking that question were facing death.

Most scholars agree that 1 Thessalonians was the earliest writing in the New Testament. That letter was very supportive, written to a church that was living in a way that pleased Paul (in contrast to most of Paul's letters, which were written to churches that were having problems). We read that Timothy had just returned to Paul from a visit to the Greek city of Thessalonica and had given a positive report. So Paul tells them to keep on doing what they are doing (4:1), and no problem arises until near the end of the epistle. The "problem" is not some misbehavior in the church but rather confusion prompted by the dying of some believers.

The early Christians had been expecting the return of Christ at any moment, and they assumed he would come while they were still alive. But Jesus's return was delayed and some Christians had died. Circumlocutions for dying and death are common. In the New Testament, it is not uncommon to refer to the state of death as "sleep" (Mark 5:39; Luke 8:52; 1 Cor. 15:51). This figurative use of "sleep" for death had long been common in Greek literature. The Thessalonians were wondering if the dead would be excluded from that final resurrection promised by Jesus. So Paul undertook to answer the question about "those who are asleep" or have "fallen asleep" (1 Thess. 4:13–15).

And what about those who were dying? The Thessalonians saw the possibility that if they did not survive until Jesus's return, they might die, and, being dead, might be out of luck when it came to the resurrection. These who were still alive and the friends and relatives of those who had "fallen asleep" already (1 Thess. 4:13) were wondering what the fate of those dead brothers and sisters might be. Picture the scene: a loved one is near death; everyone is hoping desperately for Christ's prompt return and doing their best to keep the sick person alive; some are doubtful that the person can hold on; someone suggests that they write to Paul, the founder of the church, and ask for pastoral counsel.

Whether Paul's letter arrived in time we do not know. We do know that his answer for all believers was good news. Because Jesus died and rose, he will raise all the living, dying, and dead in Christ. In fact, the dead will have priority (1 Thess. 4:16). This is not just Paul's idea, but is based on the word of the Lord (v. 15). This "word of the Lord," while not recorded in the Gospels, must have passed to Paul through some verbal transmission. It comes as a word of comfort to the dying. Was it even necessary for Paul to add verse 18, "Therefore encourage one another with these words"? "Those who are dying" (v. 13) are the center of Paul's concern.[1] The Thessalonians are in covenant with them; Jesus is with them. From the beginning, Christians have been concerned about those who are dying.

Like Paul, our goal should be to address the concerns of the dying as promptly and clearly as possible. Probably those dying or watching a loved one die will not have the same question as the Thessalonians, but they assuredly will have questions. Some may not be well formulated enough even to be expressed. But we can comprehend that they are asking the most existential and spiritual questions of their (and our) lives. These existential and spiritual questions are the ones that deal with a trajectory much longer and broader than the kinds of medical attention the sick receive; they deal not only with this life but also with what lies outside the realm of the physical life and for which our reliance on medicine and health care cannot ultimately answer.

Jesus Said . . .

The church can talk honestly about dying because Jesus not only died as we die but he also talked about it. He is the first and main dying person we are invited to hear and to speak (pray) to. He told his friends frankly that he was destined to die and he told them why and how it would happen. He talked to people whose loved ones had died and acted to alleviate their distress. We are privileged to hear his own struggles with dying, as he faced it and as he experienced it and as he had experienced it with those whom he loved. (In John 11:35, we see that he wept for the dead Lazarus.) The church can talk about dying because Scripture is never silent about it. Scripture describes Jesus's death. Scripture invites us to participate in Christ's dying.

The Jesus of the gospel story became the most important figure in the lives of the first Christians. In Jesus and what he said and did they found support, forgiveness, strength, power, hope, and love—all the things that people need to live full lives. Because Jesus provided everything these Christians needed, they began to address him in ways that expressed their appreciation of his gifts. He became "the Christ" (the one anointed by God) because of his mission; the "Son of God" because of his powers; the "Son of Man" because of his human suffering; "rabbi" or "teacher" because of his parables; "Lord" because of his authority. We base our self-understanding as Christians, as we reflected in chapter 4, on Jesus. We have already pondered some of the Christologies that reflect on Jesus's dying in ways that Christians have found helpful (such as Lamb of God and Bread of Life).

There is yet one more Christology, one more title for Jesus, that is of particular help when it comes to communicating about dying. There could be no better Christology for us at this point than that of the Word, or Word of God. This is the Jesus who himself died; he can speak to us of that. This is the Jesus who was dead; he can speak to us of that. This is the Jesus whom God raised from the dead; he can speak to us of that.

"In the beginning was the Word." So writes John, the author of the Fourth Gospel (John 1:1). He sees Jesus as God's way of communicating with humans, and he sees Jesus's language as Jesus's way of communicating to us also. Jesus as God's Word points to the wisdom and the creativity and the mind of God become human flesh. In becoming flesh and living among us, Jesus spoke to us in human language.

From the absolute beginning, God's Word was powerfully and positively creative. It was by this Word—who, as we discover in the first chapter of the Gospel of John, is Jesus— that the worlds and everything that is in them were created. Later, when the Christians wrote their story in the various documents of the New Testament, they chose to write it in Greek, the language of philosophy. In that ancient tongue, "the Word" was a term central for the writing of philosophy; it expressed reason, rationality, and orderliness. So when Jesus comes to us as the Word of God, the sense of this description includes both powerful creativity and ordered rationality— creativity controlled and powerful reason.

The fact that the life and activities and words of Jesus were written down, preserved, collected and, in effect, published as a book is still another dimension of the importance of human communication embraced by Jesus. The written word has a significance that is nearly as important as the spoken and incarnate word.

As we listen to Jesus, God's Word, communicating the loving, forgiving, reconciling nature of God to us, we are struck by the rich variety of ways in which the Word is spoken. We hear Jesus do so in a variety of styles and literary formats: commandments, prophecies, prayers, revelations, proverbs, arguments, and especially parables. He and his words occupy the central place in the Gospels. If we want to know truth, we can hear it in the words of Jesus. It comes in the most ordinary language. This fact gives us a compelling reason to

111

treat words with respect. In using ordinary human language to communicate God's truth, Jesus Christ sanctified words.

Jesus, as the Word of God, not only used ordinary language to tell God's truth; he also occasionally gave words new, special meanings. We might say that he rescued words and language from abuse by humans. We can easily see how language is used to deceive and to damage, to separate and condemn. Jesus deflated some language; he gave other, more humble vocabulary more significance. For example, he clearly downgraded and deflated language referring to the rulers of this world and upgraded servants and service. We learn that language is to be used honestly and with clarity: "Let your word be 'Yes, Yes' or 'No, No'" urged Jesus (Matt. 5:37).

Jesus's story—his life, death, and resurrection—was something new. It was astounding. Some people began to take his words seriously, remembering them and applying them, when appropriate, to their lives, and commenting upon them in written documents. This gave rise to the documents that now compose our Christian Scripture, the New Testament. Christians remembered, treasured, and lived by his words.

So what we find in Jesus, the Word, is the divine (God's) approval of the human ability to express thoughts, ideas, and emotions. Indeed, in expressing his nature in this Word (Jesus), God elevates human speech to the level of a kind of divine activity, or at least an activity that is to be undertaken with great care (Matt. 12:36). In Jesus, the Word, we find the very justification and embedded command to speak. As Jesus came to speak God's truth to all people, even to the dead (Lazarus), so we are justified and called upon not only to speak to the dying in ways that are true, life-giving, loving, and redemptive but also to speak our own concerns and hopes when we come to that end-of-life moment.

This is a Christian use of language that cannot defer to other kinds of languages that may claim to offer great benefits (e.g., medical language offering cures, popular language offering [false] courage, philosophical language offering hope

112

or acquiescence, psychological language seeking to tap inner strength).

Jesus spoke of what his death meant. In his case, of course, he saw it as something with profound implications for others; as we read that, we are particularly struck that those "others" are *us*. As the early Christian writers picked up on that theme, they unpacked his intentions in particular ways. We listen to God's word in Scripture as Jesus's dying is the cornerstone of the gospel that he was able to accomplish on our behalf. Though we have already seen examples of this in the previous chapter, more examples are found in Romans and Hebrews.

For Paul, Jesus's death put us all in the position that "whether we live or whether we die, we are the Lord's" (Rom. 14:8b). Jesus's death and life (resurrection) are connected in Paul's faith; this is because Christ, through his death and resurrection, is "Lord of both the Dead and the Living" (Rom. 14:9). Nothing, not even death, can separate us from the love of God in Jesus (Rom. 8:38–39).

For the author of the Letter to the Hebrews, Jesus died so that "he might taste death for everyone" (Heb. 2:9b), thus tying himself to every human at the point of our deepest crisis so that we might be tied to him in his triumph over death. But not only that; the author continues to say that "through [his] death he might destroy the one who has the power of death, that is, the devil" (Heb. 2:14b) so as to allay the terror of dying felt by those who were kept in fear of death. These affirmations give Christians something concrete with which to comfort one another.

But First, How Not to Communicate with the Dying

There are even more specific examples of communication about dying that Jesus provides. Some are positive examples we may use as situations seem appropriate. But some are negative, and show strategies we should not adopt when speaking to the dying. We offer them because they are typical of what many of us engage in. They were no better when Jesus was the dying person on the receiving end of ineffective communication.

Example 1: Denial. After Jesus had become aware of his impending death, he clearly and forcefully announced the prospect to his disciples (Matt. 16:21–23). He was to be judged and killed; and afterwards he would rise. This message was delivered, we are told, very clearly—no mistaking it. It was definitely a "bad news/good news" message; death was terrible news, but resurrection was astonishing, remarkable, and unexpected good news.

Despite the promise of resurrection, Peter, Jesus's lead disciple, seems to have heard only the bad news part, and he "rebuked" Jesus. We are not told his exact words, but his message to Jesus was clear: "I did not like what you said and I suggest you think differently, more positively; don't dwell on this bad stuff."

We can appreciate Peter's concern for Jesus. (Even Peter must have been aware of the deep trouble Jesus was in with the authorities and that he was in danger of being eliminated by them.) But you don't tell people facing death not to talk about it. Jesus's response to Peter is to chastise him severely: "Get behind me, Satan! You are a stumbling block to me; for you are setting your mind not on divine things, but on human things" (Matt. 16:23). He might have added, "I do want to talk about it and I want you to accept the fact."

Example 2: Failure to Be Present. After the Last Supper, when Jesus knew he was about to be arrested, he took the disciples to the garden at Gethsemane to pray about the situation. He admitted, "I am deeply grieved" (Matt. 26:38). Then he asked his disciples to watch with him while he went off to pray. They accompanied him. We don't know if they heard his prayer, but if they did they might have been surprised at his words: "My Father, if it is possible, let this cup pass

114

from me" (Matt. 26:39a). Jesus did not want to die in the way he foresaw. But perhaps the disciples did not hear; they had fallen asleep.

There they were, knowing that Jesus was facing death, and they probably wanted to do something to help. Jesus had asked them to hang around while he prayed. But instead, they fell asleep. They may not have heard the last part of his prayer either: "Yet not what I want but what you want" (Matt. 26:39b). Jesus was not pinning his hopes to escape dying on his own prayer. Instead, he was praying for the courage to continue to face what had become inevitable. Perhaps as part of that attempt to gain some courage from his friends, he went back to see them, but they had fallen asleep. He chastised them and asked them, please, to stay awake while he prayed again. When he returned to pray, though, they *again* fell asleep. This happened a total of three times. The one thing they could have done for him, they failed to do. It took no deep spiritual counsel, no excessive bravery. It only took staying there, nearby, awake. It was not much to ask.

Example 3: Change the Subject. This last bad example would be humorous if it were not in such bad taste. After Jesus gave his third forecast of his betrayal to the authorities in Jerusalem, his condemnation, crucifixion, and resurrection, he was approached by the mother of two of his disciples. She asked him, "Declare that these two sons of mine will sit, one at your right hand and one at your left, in your kingdom" (Matt. 20:21b). That was an utterly crude shift in the relationship from Jesus and his imminent death by execution to a request from a pushy mother who essentially said something like, "As soon as you are dead and raised again, will you do me the following favor?" Why couldn't she have responded to Jesus's situation with something more comforting? Instead of a response pertinent to the dreadful prospect of his death—a word of comfort, a loving embrace, a few tears of sympathy—she changed the subject to focus on her own personal agenda.

115

What the Dying Might Want to Say

In the preceding examples, Jesus spoke of his impending death; others essentially denied it, ignored him, or changed the subject. As alternatives to the preceding examples of inappropriate communications, Jesus's last words express his own human response to his dying. These are often referred to as the seven last words of Christ. The fact that Scripture preserves them for us suggests that these are examples of appropriate subjects for end-of-life discussion.

First Word: Lament (Matt. 27:46): "My God, my God, why have you forsaken me?" This is often referred to as Jesus's cry of dereliction; it communicates a sense of utter abandonment. Perhaps the most human and most universal of the dying Jesus's utterances, it could also have been his praying of Psalm 22, of which this is the first verse. It is a deeply human (and troubling) expression of hopelessness showing how fully human Jesus's experience of dying was. If this is so, and most scholars think it is, it is from one of the psalms of lament that pray for healing from sickness (others are Pss. 6; 38; 39; 41; 88; and 102). These psalms are providentially in Scripture to provide those in desperate situations the means and the encouragement to voice their complaints directly to God. The existence of the psalms and the use of one of them by the dying Jesus provide additional assurance that we cannot be separated from God even in the most extreme circumstances. When Jesus—or anyone else—uses a lament to attack, blame, or simply shout at God, he is doing so because he believes God ought to be there with him and has betrayed his divine character by being absent.[2] By not taking advantage of such laments in addressing the needs of the dying, Allen Verhey observes, "we obscure the hurtful realities of human experience and drive both suffering and response to suffering outside the practice of our faith. Thus we marginalize not only suffering but also sufferers. When we make so little room in liturgy for lament, then in their hurt and their anger and their sense of absurdity, sufferers think they sit alone in the congregation."[3] Using the lament is a way to "encompass the hurt within a faithful identity."[4]

Second Word: Forgive (Luke 23:34): "Father, forgive them; for they do not know what they are doing." This is an extraordinary moment, and yet we know that the dying want to resolve outstanding grievances and *heal broken relationships.* With this prayer for forgiveness, Jesus seems to echo that normal human need for forgiveness and resolution. He will not take anger or recrimination into death.

Third Word: Offer Hope (Luke 23:43): "Truly I tell you, today you will be with me in Paradise." Jesus continued his ministry in the midst of his own dying by *promising hope* to the repentant criminal crucified alongside him. The dying Jesus has no reason not to tell the truth; he has every reason to promote hope.

Fourth Word: Express Physical Needs (John 19:28): "I am thirsty." Jesus had *physical needs* and did not hesitate to express them. The Gospel writers did not shy away from the "corruption of the flesh," even when they referred to Jesus, who was to be their Lord.

Fifth Word: Address the Needs of Others (John 19:26–27): "Woman, here is your son. . . . Here is your mother." Jesus "takes care of business" as a son and as a friend. We do not know the status of Jesus's mother, Mary, but if she was a widow, she would need the care of a male relative in that cultural time and place. Jesus is clearly thinking of that as he "assigns" his beloved disciple, John, to assume the role of a son to his surviving mother. Even the dying can take care of business on a level consistent with their energy and alertness. Jesus never stopped thinking of others.

Sixth Word: Commit the Self to God (Luke 23:46): "Father, into your hands I commend my spirit." Jesus is cognizant of his impending death and signals that he is now about to die. These words suggest that his final thought is not the anxious one of the first word of dereliction but rather of a

117

final reconciliation that death is upon him and as a final decision to *entrust himself* and whatever awaits him to God the Father. This is the ultimate word of faith: the dying person makes his final decision and for Jesus it is the decision to entrust all to God.

Seventh Word: Accept the End (John 19:30): "It is finished." These are words of human suffering and of the conclusion of a life's work. These words are not so different from the concerns that we are told that the dying have. This is a statement of *resolution* of pending concerns and the *acceptance* of death.

This language was the right kind of language. It was not evasive. It was not Pollyannaish. It was about dying—what everyone there was actually thinking about. It was the real language of a real person experiencing real dying. The dying Jesus has things to say that are helpful. Can we, when we die, speak helpfully to others? If so, what could we say?

A Christian practice of using language truthfully and lovingly is a first step toward providing a ministry to the dying. We know words are powerful for good and for ill. In a remarkable autobiographical glimpse into his own dying of cancer, Joseph Cardinal Bernardin, the Roman Catholic archbishop, insisted that, as spiritual leader of the two million Catholics in his Chicago archdiocese, he was obligated to let them know his condition. Far from concealing or at least not discussing the matter, Bernardin gave full disclosure of his condition to his flock so that they would not feel abandoned by him.[5]

The story is told of a patient who read all she could about her condition and would try to discuss her newly acquired knowledge with her doctors. At first they felt that she was critical of their care for her. At one session, after spending hours reading about the latest research on treatments for her illness, she said to the care team, "Now I understand how difficult your job is." Her positive understanding of her clinicians' challenges turned out to be greatly supportive of them.[6]

If we can live in Christ and acknowledge our need to be formed as Christians, "the core of spiritual formation that emerges from a life lived practicing God's presence at least provides a language and a worldview [a narrative] that enable a person to begin to make sense of his or her suffering"[7] in end-of-life situations. That means that when one has been "spiritually formed," one has experienced disciplining that creates the habits, thoughts, and practices of faithfulness, concern for others, and patience with life that can be used in times of affliction. If the church can truly be the "community of communication,"[8] as it is meant to be, the corps of those prepared for difficulties should be neither few nor weak.

Christian Use of Language

What difference does Jesus as the Word of God make for us, as his disciples? As is the case with his dying and our response in baptism, does it not make new persons of us? Does it not make us servants of Jesus the Word, of the words of Jesus, and the words of Scripture? First of all, the fact that Jesus is God's Word makes us respecters of language and of clear communication. We are obligated with a marvelous opportunity: we are called and empowered by God to speak the truth helpfully to all.

It has been said that our world, the world accessible to each of us individually, is limited by the language we use. One language confines us to one narrow world (for example, if it is English, only to English-speaking people and cultures). Two languages expand the world in which we can live. Learning the Christian faith is all about learning a new language, one with a new vocabulary that will change the way in which we observe and describe our world. "Vocabulary is everything," writes Stanley Hauerwas. "Few tasks are more important in our day than teaching the language of the faith. But . . . the language must be constitutive of the work to be done. It is not as if the language is a means to do the work, but the *language is the work to be done.*"[9] So Christians really need a second first language—the language of the gospel, the language of the kingdom, the language of the good news story of God's love for each of us.

This is theological language, but don't fear it. It is part of our work as Christians to be clear about our theology of dying. This is the language of what God has done and how we have experienced it. It is the language of the concrete specifics of God's grace. It is language that may seem technical, obscurantist, and elitist to a person without faith, but it is a language that is a better vehicle for the precision that the person of faith needs to carry the burden of meaning. Just as the physician needs to say "Simvastatin" rather than "that rose-colored pill" and the auto mechanic fares far better calling for the "air filter" than "that big round thing," so the dying Christian can better respond to the promise of God's grace and the awe of God's holiness than have nothing concrete to say when identifying his understanding of God.

Our Christian language is the language of God's power, God's love for God's own creation, God's long-suffering and mercy, God's judgment, and God's will for the creation. Christian language has a peculiar sound because it is the language of sin and redemption, of judgment and grace. These are words of hope and confidence. This Christian language is a confident one, even when speaking of dying.[10]

Beginning with Jesus, a whole new language emerged: Christian language. It was needed to tell the Christian story because the Christian story was a new and different one. There are many literary formats—letters, gospels, psalms, histories, genealogies, songs, poems—that together make up the Scriptures that convey this new story.

We enter into this Christian story and find it makes more sense to us than other stories we have heard. As Christians, we should think of ourselves as bilingual, working in the world with one language and living the Christian life with a richer, larger, more powerful, more penetrating language that makes more sense because it explains more of life in a more honest and helpful and meaningful way. That is good news.

The good news is that it is language that opens up to us rich meanings and insights into the nature of God, the meaning of life, and the world around. Christians have been given a language that is special in that it expresses things that others may not yet know. As God's Word, Jesus used and has formed language so that we are now transformed by it. Of course, not everyone speaks that language. So there is a special burden on Christians to take language seriously. Indeed, as we build our theology of dying, we may need terminology that expresses truths and realities that the language of our secular world, our medical establishment, or our cultural environment is unable to provide, simply because we are talking about things that God has revealed to us in Jesus Christ.

Christian vocabulary is at once both specialized and general. It is specialized in that it relies on terms specific to it to express the unique features of faith: humans as *creature*s of God, human *sin*, God's *grace*. Such terms are specific to faith but ignored by other jargons (medical jargon, for instance). For this it is criticized as sectarian or confined to a (falsely perceived) narrow religious sphere of life. But it is precisely with those special terms that such language is able to name features of the human experience that other languages cannot name, such as "sin" and "grace." Christians need their own language in order to say the wonderfully new and different message they believe, because what they believe is in many ways countercultural, and the communication vehicle of modern American culture is not adequate to bear the weight and express the nuances of the Christian faith. But this Christian "jargon" is not private. It refers to the reality of all human experience.

Christian language is not a "jive" vocabulary current with some new cultural fad or a dialect that appeared in some previously undiscovered backwater of the world. Ours is an old vocabulary, rooted in the Word of God made flesh in Jesus

Christ. It goes back still further, fashioned first among the ancient Israelites as they reflected on their experience with a God who saved them from slavery and made them into a blessed and blessing nation. Our vocabulary was quickened by the Christian experience with the risen Christ and enriched as Christians moved out from Palestine into the wider world, where that vocabulary was tested and refined as Christians encountered, and explained themselves to, other peoples with other languages. Ours is a powerful language into whose simple words and phrases are packed understandings of immense power and consequence, fabulous riches and promises, and terrifying critiques and judgments. As it developed throughout the past two thousand years, millions of believers have used it to deepen their own faith and to explain themselves and their faith to others.

Christians' Powerful Vocabulary: Seven Examples

Ours is neither an insular nor an insulating language. It is too old and universal for that. It has a powerful vocabulary that is worth a brief review in order to remind us of its scope and its applicability to the end-of-life experience. This is a vocabulary not really owned by mainstream American culture and not relied on in the communications that occur at end of life. Let us examine some of the words that can be constructively used in our conversations with and about the dying.

1. Creation. We are creatures. That means we are made by someone or something else. The universe and all that is in it is "creature"; that is, it is *made.* We believe that the maker, that source, is God and that the creation was not only made by God, but made good and made for a purpose. We are not in charge of anything; we are only servants dedicated to the care of what (and who) there is. What there is is good and demands our care, whether it is our own bodies, other (*all* other) people, the whole of nature, or a speck in the farthest corner of outer space. What there is is conditional, not necessary; it is transitory, not permanent but liable to death. The created, physical world, wonderful as it is, changes and ultimately will be gone. We cannot ultimately rely on any permanence from it. If we long for what is permanent, then the created world, the world we know around us, is not what we should seek. We need to seek the Maker, the Creator, God.

2. *Eschatology.* This refers to purpose and gives us a word to affirm that there is a purpose in God's creation, and that in achieving that purpose the world as we know it is going to end and be replaced by whatever it is that God might have in mind for later. So whatever it is we are about stands under an ultimate judgment beyond any judgment known to our own understanding. This is a crucial source of hope both to the dying and to those who will be left behind. To know that there is both meaning and purpose in our individual lives and in the life of the cosmos provides an assurance that is impossible to acquire without the purposeful death and meaningful resurrection of Jesus.

3. *Forgiveness.* "I don't get mad, I get even" reads the bumper sticker. According to American culture, forgiveness is a sign either of weakness or stupidity. But forgiveness is one of the fundamental characteristics of the God who self-reveals to us in faith. This is an astonishing characteristic, particularly in the fact that we ourselves can be forgiven for our fall, sin, or transgression (call the problem what you will). We pray about this in the Lord's Prayer; we confess its reality in the Apostles' Creed. To the extent that this characteristic becomes characteristic of us, the astonishment continues. Here is a behavior, an attitude, that is almost totally lacking in secular culture, whether at the individual level or the level of international relationships.

How can this be a resource? Those who know forgiveness in their own lives know the liberation they experience because of it. Those who practice forgiveness toward others know the lightening of their own load of ill will. Forgiveness is something that helps the forgiver and the forgiven. Here is another word that describes a reality that can be known only in the naming of it. One of the most commonly mentioned problems faced by the dying is that of unsettled relationships and unresolved disputes. These situations call for resolution, particularly in the form of forgiveness. It is a matter of tidying up the last loose ends and in many cases (because of illness and weakness) it is about the only thing that a dying person can do: to either offer or accept forgiveness, or do both.

4. *Grace*. Here is a word that has virtually disappeared from American English. In Christian usage it refers to a number of things from prayer before meals to God's sending of Jesus Christ for the salvation of the world. It, like forgiveness, is a characteristic of God. It can also be a powerful gift that the dying can dispense. In acting with grace, God is not just behaving in a fine manner; God is always moving toward us, though without force, in love and forgiveness, offering us what we need. God precedes us when necessary because we don't always acknowledge our need. He follows to clean up after us when necessary. Grace is a resource for the dying because it is the infinite capacity of God to do the right thing for us.

5. *Sin*. The New Testament Greek word for sin is something like "missing the mark," as when an archer shoots and misses the target. It is an appropriate term to describe the human condition. Here we are, failing at what God created us for: creative and intimate fellowship with one another. Instead, we want to re-create ourselves *for* ourselves; we compete, we don't cooperate; we destroy, we don't create; we want more and different and are not satisfied with the givenness of who we are. We not only sin, but we have created (and a perverse kind of creation it is!) a sinful environment for human life. The world is tainted with our sin and we cannot run from it.

"Sin" is a term often misused. *Sin* is a word properly used for the condition into which we place ourselves. Secular misuse is found in the popular and fragmented use of the term "sins." Then these little pieces (sins) can be reduced

124

and sanitized ("Gossip isn't all that bad"; "I couldn't resist the urge to . . . [whatever]").

"Sin" is what everybody does and has; "sinful" is what everybody is. This is a nondiscriminatory, equal-opportunity, self-inflicted failure of the human condition. It is not our intended condition; that original condition was good (Gen. 1:31). But now we are sinful; that is not good and it is our own fault. The naming of sin is a powerful thing. Sin may capture the sense of exactly what it is that a dying person needs to get rid of. Sin was the main thing the dying (and resurrected) Jesus attended to. The pain and uncertainties present at the end of life can be one more occasion or opportunity for us to ignore or deny God, but God is available even then to forgive and accept.

6. *Gospel.* This is the word that summarizes all of the good news God provides for us in Christ. Is there any good that we can find in (this) dying? The beatitude for the dead and dying in Revelation 14:13 has a promise. They are blessed; they will rest from their labors; their work is done, and their deeds are neither forgotten nor lost.

7. *Resurrection.* The popular cultural tendency is to believe in a kind of guaranteed and automatic immortality. That is not the Christian understanding. Christians take death very seriously and have since the time of Jesus when any idea of a resurrection of the dead was a far-off hope. The resurrection of Jesus was an astonishing event. It did not install a regime of immortality, but rather was only the first of a new creation, one in which God would raise the dead. There is nothing in humans that automatically survives death. There is only the power and grace of God that showed that his love overcame death. The hope for an innate immortality can lead to a trivialization of death. Christians are aware of the seriousness and threat of physical death. Instead of hoping that there is some seed of immortality within themselves that will guarantee a safe passage to a "better place," the Christian throws all his or her hopes onto the God whose power

created all that there is and whose power can be trusted to raise again that which dies.

These are only seven of the words unique to the Christian faith that name realities Christians experience and help us speak of our own faith experiences clearly and precisely. These seven words affirm and clarify ways and content of Christian talk in end-of-life situations. We are reminded that we are creatures, not our own and not just God's, but related in a sacred covenant and web of intertwined personal stories to others. All things work together for good for those who love God (Rom. 8:28). There is purpose to be found in all of our moments. Forgiveness is available for each of us and for others through us. God's grace is what enables this to occur, even in difficult moments. Recognition of sin, ours and that of others, is a recognition of hard reality, but there is good news (gospel) because God is with us with the power of resurrection, a triumph after death.

Discussion Questions

1. If you feel awkward conversing with someone you know to have a terminal illness, why do you think that you feel that way?
2. If you were facing death from a terminal illness, how would you like others to treat you?
3. Alone or in a group, develop a list of questions that you—if you knew you were soon to die—would want to have answered. (Who might be the most likely source for answers? Are these questions that you would be afraid to ask? Do you think your minister would be interested in preaching a sermon on each question?)
4. Role-play some scenes in which one person assumes the role of a terminally ill person; another the role of the minister; another the role of a clinician; and others random friends, relatives, or acquaintances. Invent

scenes in which conversations occur between and among various players. The point of this exercise might first be to break the ice in just talking. Later, after a number of repetitions, the group members should increase in comfort and sensitivity in all the different roles involved and become more frank in expressing their ideas and feelings.

6

Preaching on Death and Dying

Death as an event activates certain rituals and words of caring in the family and in the church, but dying as a process also draws to itself rituals and words for the one dying, the family, and the church. However, when the process of dying is not acknowledged, awkward silence and fumbling inactivity may result when death is announced, leaving all concerned welcoming the chance to do something they know how to do: visit a funeral director, prepare a memorial service, or perhaps plan meals for out-of-towners and the grieving family.

Should the pulpit wait until death arrives to say an appropriate word? Is death a subject appropriate for the pulpit?[1] Of course, when a member of the congregation dies, the occasion calls for the minister to speak of the deceased, either in the sanctuary of the church or in the chapel of the funeral home. Most ministers possess a manual containing familiar and favorite texts of Scripture, prayer, poems, and hymns, usefully organized with some specificity: death of a child, death of an elderly person, death of a soldier, death by accident, death by suicide, and so forth. It is unfortunate that the manual saves some ministers from having to think, struggle, and pray in order for the memorial service to be appropriate for and unique to the deceased. But whatever the pastoral habits of the minister, it goes without saying that persons will die, memorial services will be held, and words about death will be spoken. But the question is, should a sermon about death be preached when no one is dead, when the congregation has gathered for its usual Sunday worship? Mind you, we are not thinking of such a sermon for shock value or in the service of evangelism or stewardship or for any other program, but as a subject on the pastor's regular pulpit menu.

Some say no to preaching such a sermon, and do so for various reasons. Such sermons, they say, are too difficult for the listener and open old wounds and stir sad memories, sending some worshipers early to the exits. Delivering such sermons is difficult, and is especially so if the church is generally silent about death. But rather than expecting *more* silence, we should encourage *less* silence, setting such sermons within a larger conversation in the church and sharing the resources of the faith in various contexts and not in worship alone. In this way the subject of death can gather rather than scatter.

Some ministers say no to such sermons simply because maintaining silence is easier. Most of the time silence is easier than speaking. Talking about important matters is always difficult. Have you talked to your spouse about this? Your parents? Your children? No, I'm waiting for it to come up naturally so we will be totally at ease. And when will that be? Of course, conversations and sermons on important and critical subjects make us nervous; that is the way the body registers the significance of the occasion. To paraphrase Shakespeare, we draw our breath in pain to tell the story.

And if someone objects to sermons on death and dying with the argument that the pulpit is for good news not bad news, remind that person that silence on the subject is not good news. Good news is addressing pain, suffering, and loss, speaking to the dark places and bringing light from the Creator and Redeemer, the God of love and life. Someone needs to toss a word at the clear glass of silence and release conversation into the room. And that person is usually the preacher. If the pulpit is silent, the congregation is usually silent, and in that silence hurt is not healed but deepened and extended.

Think about one not-so-unique case of silence. A man seemingly strong dies suddenly of a heart attack. A family has lost a husband, a father, a brother; and a ten-year-old boy has lost a favorite uncle. Family and friends gather, in silence. Food is brought by the church, in silence. A funeral is held and the body is buried, in silence. The nephew is silent, retreating to his room. He returns to school, in silence. He does not talk at home or at school. His silence continues for days, weeks, or perhaps months. No parents, friends, teachers, or counselors can break the silence. Finally, at the family table, the nephew cries uncontrollably, blurting out his judgment on everyone there, "Nobody loved Uncle Howard; no one cried; no one said anything." It was true that they had been silent, agreeing among themselves that they would not mourn in front of the children, for fear of upsetting them. However, it was the silence that was painfully upsetting. In the face of dying and death, the silence must be broken. It is reasonable to expect the conversation to begin with the preacher. How might the preacher begin? In no particular order, here are a few suggestions.

Assume Familiarity with Death

Assume that all your listeners are acquainted with death. What the pulpit has to say on the subject does not come as breaking news, not even to the children. They are already asking questions: Do hamsters go to heaven? Will Grandma stay dead long? The youth have lost friends in twisted steel and broken glass. Sooner rather than later, death will visit the hospital and nursing home, whisking away the elderly. And sometimes, on quiet feet, death will slip into the nursery and hush the whimpering child. Everyone hearing a sermon will have some acquaintance with death.

Assume Listeners Want to Hear about Death from the Church

Assume also that all your listeners want to hear about death from the church and in the church. They hear of it plenty from cynics who make their hearts a desert and call it peace, from melancholy poets who love the darkness, from the bored who play at the edges of suicide, from the shallow heads who show up at every funeral wearing a bright badge that announces "Smile, God loves you." In spite of all its failings, the church carries in its heart and in its mouth a Word from God for those who die and those who bury them. The church carries in its chest of memories resources adequate and bold enough to speak of life and joy and hope at the very time those blessings seem to have been stolen. It is not a word easily spoken, a word readily available on demand, or a word looking like a happy greeting. It is a word drawn in pain and moist with tears. But it is a strong word that, when spoken, challenges dread, fear, denial, and superstition. It is a clear word, not disguising itself in vague and generic vocabulary, such as "mortality" and "immortality." It announces not that "all are mortal" but that "Mae Pearson died this morning about six o'clock after a tough battle with pneumonia." The word is shocking, but not altogether surprising. Death has its forerunners: the loss of a job, the moving van in front of a good neighbor's house, the turning of leaves to flame, the empty nest. All such experiences carry a hint of death.

And so we both want and don't want our minister to preach on death. We are both ready and never ready to hear that sermon. But the silence is hurtful and harmful, so break it, please. The preacher who, having been invited to speak in the chapel service at West Point, decided to preach about death did not deserve the flood of mail criticizing his decision. His choice was appropriate, and his message was drawn from the deep resources of the Christian faith. It was a word from the God of life and love and hope.

Think Through Your Own Theology of Death and Dying

Let the preacher think through his or her own theology as it bears on death and dying. This does not mean that one's views are fixed and clear and adequate for a lifetime of preaching, but it does mean that the preacher is not exempt personally from the question death brings to faith. It also means that the preacher accepts the fact that the clergy has no resources for dealing with death that are unavailable to the congregation. But the preacher can model how the resources of Scripture, tradition, hymns, prayers, experience, and the lives of saints past and present can be woven into faith and faithfulness adequate for the times when death appears to be the only reality. One does not have to appear invulnerable and certain, but one's preaching on death must carry the marks of struggle to a point of serenity. The minister always at war with himself or herself on this as well as other issues of faith will often make casualties of the listeners. Or, to change the image, the parishioners do not expect that the pastor has already arrived at the end of faith's journey, but they do need evidence that the pastor is on the journey and has traveled far enough to help them with their questions. And they will have questions. Sometimes it may be a question that seems as semicynical, semicomical as that put to Jesus: If a woman were to marry in succession seven brothers, in the resurrection whose wife will she be? (Luke 20:27–40). Jesus listened to the question and used the occasion to teach about God. Sometimes it may be a question growing out of congregational dispute: If those still alive when Christ returns are raptured, what happens to our members already dead and buried? (1 Thess. 4:13–18). Paul was patient with the congregation, answering, teaching, and encouraging. Probably the most frequently asked questions have to do with whether or not there is a direct correlation between one's faith and the banes or blessings of one's life. This question arises when a saint suffers and a nonbeliever flourishes. Jesus faced this question, not answering it on the surface but answering the larger issue of life before God (Luke 13:1–5). The author of Hebrews deals with the question by acknowledging that "by faith" some were successful and victorious over every enemy (Heb. 11:32–35a) while others "by faith" were tortured, tormented, exiled, and killed (Heb. 11:35b–38). Such texts can help the dying and the grieving move past guilt ("I must not have enough faith") and anger ("Life isn't fair; the world is out of joint"). Preaching on death and dying will not eliminate these and other questions but sermons on these texts lay the groundwork for more substantive conversation when death does enter the church.

Thinking through one's theology about death will also relieve ministry to the dying and the grieving of other common errors. For example, one does not argue theology at such times. Expect the desperate and frantic to grasp at anything with the promise of answers. To the anxious, even old superstition and homegrown theology may look helpful. The situation calls for patience and understanding, not superior theology. If the dying hope for a miracle, it is no time to announce that one does not believe in miracles. After all, how can one believe in God and at the same time shut the door to divine activity? The preacher does not walk through the waiting room, which the church is sometimes, snatching away hope. And the preacher does not, publicly or privately, speak against the attending medical caregivers. By and large, they are as committed to their tasks as the preacher is to his or hers. The clergy are not physicians; the physicians are not clergy. Coming to clarity about such matters before death occurs serves the preacher well when the phone does ring.

Steep Your Words in Scripture

To say again what has been touched upon already, let the preacher share fully in sermons the biblical texts that permit, even demand, preparation for death and dying and that serve as resources for ministry when these critical times do come. It is not enough that the congregation be told what the preacher thinks about this or that; rather, the congregation needs to be in conversation with the Scriptures. The Bible is the church's book, and it is the preacher's task to give the church its Bible as helpfully as possible. This is achieved, not by gathering verses from hither and thither under headings such as "What the Bible Says About . . ." To accumulate texts in this manner is to be seduced by the concordance, and for the overwhelmed listener it is "piling on." The Bible is really not one book but a library, addressing different readers at different times and places and for a variety of reasons. It is more respectful of the Bible to listen in on each text as it is read without effort to make it agree with other texts. Let it say what it wants to say.

This is the manner in which the preacher will bring biblical resources to bear on death and dying. Naturally, not all texts deal with this subject, but those that do can be heard on any Sunday morning. Listeners will, over time, have deposits in their memory banks sufficient to equip them for the hours of death and dying. What could be more helpfully appropriate than the portrayal of Jesus's full identification with us in tears, suffering, and death that we find in Hebrews (5:7–8)? Or Paul's image of his own approaching death as a libation being poured out on the altar of the church's faith (Phil. 2:17–18)? Or who would not be instructed as well as moved by Paul's remembering not only old friends but also the families of friends deceased (Rom. 16:10–11)? No doubt, a time of silence followed the reading of Paul's letter to the church in Rome. Or is there any more fitting description of the way life is for a believer than Paul's experience of diminishing physical energy while at the same time having increasing vigor of spirit (2 Cor. 4:16)? And, of course, the primary interest of the church is in what Jesus says of suffering and death. When he thought his friends were able to hear it, Jesus talked to them about his approaching death (Mark 8:31). All of us resonate with the sharp words of Martha to Jesus: "If you had been here, my brother would not have died" (John 11:21). And all of us try to claim his promise that the one who believes does not face judgment but already has eternal life, having passed from death to life (John 5:24). And if anyone asks whether Jesus ever spoke at a funeral, read and talk about Jesus's eulogy for John the Baptist, a prisoner but not yet dead (Luke 7:18–35). Luke apparently believed eulogies should precede rather than follow death. Recall his story of Paul delivering his own eulogy to the elders of the Ephesian church in a meeting at Miletus (Acts 20:17–38). We need not continue this matter; the preacher who lives daily in the Scriptures will have no lack of resources in order to preach and sustain a congregational conversation on the subject of death and dying. And let all of us who preach remember that we were not called to explain what our forebears proclaimed but to proclaim what they proclaimed.

Enlist the Congregation

Ministers will not, of course, forget that they work in the context of a congregation, a community. The minister is the only professional in town with a congregation: physicians have patients, lawyers have clients, businessmen have customers, but only the minister has a congregation. The minister does not work alone; the congregation rejoices with those who rejoice and weeps with those who weep. Many besides the clergy have gifts appropriate to the needs of those who suffer and who die. The congregation is an irreplaceable source of energy, support, and understanding. After all, death and dying are social events, and isolation from the caring community of faith means isolation from one of the primary sources of healing, of comfort, and of dying well. Preventing such isolation requires initiative and sustained attention by the church; otherwise, the habit of the culture to hide away the ill and dying will take over.

Reminders of this fact can properly come from the pulpit. This does not call for special announcements (although not out of order) but for weaving appropriately into sermons reminders of the corporate nature of the Christian life. We are members of one another. The reciprocal pronoun, translated "one another," is essential, not optional, in the biblical story. The screaming demoniac called Legion, isolated by his community, is restored to that community. The isolated leper is readmitted to family and community. The woman with a hemorrhage is restored to her home and community. This is to say, the healthy condition for each person is to be a member of a community, and a part of Jesus's healing was mending broken relationships. The minister and the congregation know that, speak of it often, and work to see that it is so. At one level, this involves shared information about each other. At a deeper level, our lives are interwoven, in sickness and in health. Seldom will such a condition exist if the pulpit is silent.

Lead in Lament

Finally, the pulpit can well take the lead in providing congregational laments. There are, of course, personal and family laments, usually spontaneous, private, or semiprivate, and often wordless, raw emotion. But the congregation as a congregation needs to lament. The time and place can well be a regular worship service. The minister can help the congregation understand both the form and the content of a lament. The psalmist led Israel in laments; the prophets gave voice to the people's lamentation. In the New Testament, Revelation 18 is a lament. The minister can lead in understanding that laments are acts of worship with a particular form. There is no contradiction between "formal" and "from the heart." An entire service may be a lament or a self-contained unit of a service may be a lament. Such a service provides an occasion for expressing anger toward God, questioning God's goodness or power to help, expressing sorrow and regret, confessing sin and weakness, and renewing vows of love and commitment. The service is honest in its expression but always worshipful toward God. The minister speaks for self and for the people. But the people also speak, and pray, and sing.

Laments would be appropriate at such times as the congregation feels keenly disruptive, intrusive, and almost unbearable loss. The minister and the congregation will know when that time has come. It is the time when pretense is forbidden and all pitch in to help put faith together again. It is the time when "He is not here" seems the last word until we are able to say again, "He is risen."

Discussion Questions

1. Could funeral sermons be sufficient for preaching to address issues of dying? Argue both the pros and cons.
2. List and discuss any reasons why pastors do not preach on texts that portray dying, on the topic or theme of dying, or on subjects that relate to dying.
3. If you were to design a sermon (or a series of sermons!) that would address end-of-life issues, what might it look like? (What biblical texts? How would Jesus Christ be presented? What cultural conventions would be engaged? What would be avoided?)

7

Facing Dying Faithfully

A Small Cloud of Witnesses

Chapters 1 and 2 laid out the problem: Christians and their churches may live the faith well, but do not do as well when it comes to dying. Chapters 3, 4, 5, and 6 remind us of the resources available in the story of Jesus Christ, in the transformed lives of Christians, in the power for truthful communication, and in the public voice of the church.

Throughout the whole history of Christendom, the church has always been sensitive to the needs of the dying faithful, and in each age specific official and popular resources have been available and offered to aid those facing end-of-life issues. In the earliest period, when being a Christian was politically hazardous, being a Christian was also rigorously demanding. The mere choice to be a believer meant that one's commitment included a sure and enthusiastic confidence in the resurrection.

Once the church became dominant and its power was that of the Roman Empire, it focused on the liturgical and ritual exercises by which the church "guaranteed" a safe passage into the next life. But in time profound changes altered the spiritual landscape and the church expanded the breadth of resources available to Christians as they faced dying. The most important of these new resources was a kind of manual, *The Art of Dying (ars moriendi)*, written in the early 1400s and circulated widely for centuries in various versions. This offered directions, encouragement, chastisement, and assurances about dying and how to prepare to meet the creator and judge. The *ars moriendi* tradition sustained Christians in the face of dying down to the beginnings of modern times.

The power of the church to provide what Peter Berger calls a "plausibility structure,"[1] a way of thinking that ensured the certainty of the Christian message, and particularly its understanding of death and dying, faltered. In chapters 3–6 we have reminded the reader of the resources of Scripture and Christology and have offered them in broad outline. But there are no longer any "how-to-do-it" plans for dying well as there had been with the *ars moriendi* tradition.

There is no recipe for mixing the ingredients of Christology, Scripture, and theology into a guaranteed salve that will eliminate the utterly serious and often painful end-of-life struggle that is coping with dying. We have reminded the reader of the resources, too often ignored, that are in plain sight in the tradition of the Christian faith. They must be actualized in each life in ways that incarnate God's love for each individual creature. What we have brought to memory in the preceding chapters does not constitute the one procrustean version of the Christian narrative into which we are all finally expected to settle. That has dangers that are avoidable.[2] Their application is up to us.

Since "the deceased remain a part of the Christian community,"[3] the dying can teach the living.[4] Gathered in this chapter is an assortment of thoughts from fellow Christians who have died. What distinguishes them from most who have died is that they have left us written accounts of their thoughts about dying. Perhaps in such accounts we may find models and paths to consider as we make our own preparations for dying.

What follows are snapshots into the lives of ten Christians who have left some written record of their spiritual odysseys toward the end of life. These stories contrast in important ways from the ten pastors of chapter 1. We do not devalue the faith or witness of the pastors of chapter 1, but different end-of-life choices might have led them and their congregations to better dyings. The examples cited in this chapter are offered for the reader's use, in whatever way(s) they might be helpful—in personal devotional contemplation, in preaching, in discussion groups, in the study of church history, or in the facing of one's own death.

The examples date from the first to the twentieth centuries; there are men and women, Catholics and Protestants, those passionate in faith or struggling in doubt, some activists and some contemplatives. These differences are important because they demonstrate that coping with dying as a Christian is definitely not a "one-size-fits-all" strategy; more important, those discussed below all find their help in the same tradition we have reviewed in the previous chapters. And all of them are united in believing that dying can be faced faithfully and with a hopeful outcome. They all find their focus in Jesus Christ.

Each thumbnail biography appears in much the same format so that the individuality of each is clear, and clearly distinguished from the others. The biographical sketch includes a focus on the specific concern, commitment, or crisis that prompted the urgency of a serious consideration of dying, their theology of dying, the specific resources utilized, and the helpful legacy left behind for the church to consider. This will provide an opportunity for the reader to see the similarities and differences and most easily to consider ways of adding these biographical resources to the theology of dying already given us in Jesus Christ.

The intent is not to offer the reader a collection of success stories about good deaths. Actually, we do not know how these believers died.[5] Nor does the theology of dying developed throughout chapters 3–5 appear explicitly or systematically in any of the stories. That is perfectly understandable since the engagement with end-of-life concerns of the following writers has often been existential and always individual, and none seem to have been concerned to spell out a consistent construct in an organized and complete manner.

However, it is possible to gain confidence from the testimony of others, and there may be a voice in the following stories that captures and inspires one to pursue the same hope for a good dying. Perhaps seeing the variety of ways one may grapple with end-of-life challenges will stimulate readers to embrace and use faith's resources in original and helpful ways. Perhaps one or another of these stories will stimulate conversations about Christian coping with dying that can serve the wider Christian community.

Paul (?–65 CE?): To Live Is Christ; To Die Is Gain

The apostle Paul is probably the best known of our examples. He was an early convert from Judaism to the Christian faith. As Christianity became a universal faith, Paul found he was called to be a missionary with the responsibility of taking the Christian gospel to the world outside of Judaism. The central points of that gospel were that Jesus was the Christ promised by God to reconcile a broken world and that Christ would be soon returning from heaven to establish the kingdom of God. In the course of his ministry, Paul founded churches around the northeastern rim of the Mediterranean in countries we know today as Syria, Turkey, and Greece. After establishing those churches, he kept in contact with them, offering support and advice to meet the challenges they encountered. Paul was a bachelor (free from family obligations), a tent maker (he could support himself wherever his ministry took him), and a Roman citizen (which gave him legal protection not afforded to many Christians).

What drove Paul was the passion to bring everyone to belief in Christ before Christ's expected return to earth.

What did Paul think about his own dying? Though he did not live under a sentence of death as did Jesus and several of the individuals profiled below, he did experience some life-threatening moments that would have caused him to consider that his death was imminent: he was beaten eight times (with lashes, with rods), stoned, shipwrecked three times (including a day and night spent adrift at sea), and endured several imprisonments (2 Cor. 11:23–25). This is in addition to other hazards: danger from rivers, robbers, Jews, and Gentiles (2 Cor. 11:26), persecution (2 Cor. 4:9), afflictions, hardships, calamities, tumults, and hunger (2 Cor. 6:4–5). He considered himself near death many times (2 Cor. 11:23). But he treats these life-threatening situations as trivial. In fact, to him, life or death is a "six of one, a half dozen of the other" kind of choice. He writes that "to live is Christ and to die is gain" (Phil. 1:21 NIV).

What were the resources upon which he may have drawn to come to an almost cavalier attitude toward dying? They certainly differed dramatically from those available to us. He did not have any New Testament documents; he was one of the ones who wrote them! He did have access, however, to some of the eyewitnesses to the life, words, works, death, and resurrection of Jesus. For example, in 1 Thessalonians 4:15 he writes of a "word of the Lord" that assured believers that both those living and those dying or already dead would participate in the resurrection whenever Jesus returned. That "word" is not found in our Gospels; we would not have heard it unless Paul had received it through the church's oral tradition and written it in a letter.

Another resource, and the one that provided strength to his attitude, was the intense conviction that Jesus would soon return and usher in the kingdom of God, the reality at the heart of Jesus's (and Paul's) ministry (Phil. 1:10; 4:5; 1 Thess. 1:10; 3:13; 5:23). Because of that conviction, he was totally committed to gather in all people to Christ's body before that final event occurred.

His focus on his work—to get it done before Christ returns—seems to have ironed out every possible hindrance, threat, and obstacle (Rom. 8:38). Nothing could come between Paul and Christ, including death. That was because Jesus was Lord of both the Living and the Dead. Death therefore did not constitute a moment of crisis for Paul; he was concerned about other matters. The sufferings and hazards he experienced were a part of his experience with Christ. Christ was "in" him to the point where his own resurrection was assured and in the process his own sufferings were considered a sharing in the sufferings of Christ (2 Cor. 1:5; Col. 1:24).

Since Christ is Lord of both the Living and the Dead (1 Thess. 5:10; Rom. 14:9), Paul may have seen dying as merely a transition for himself in passing from one state to the other. He disregarded dying as a hazard. Better said, he regarded it as irrelevant. He mentioned it in a list of things that could not separate him from God (Rom. 8:38) and asserted that he could be fine under any circumstances (Phil. 4:11–13). In fact, life and death seemed the same (Phil. 1:21; 2:14–18) and sometimes he even indicated that he would prefer death (2 Cor. 5:8). He certainly would have liked to have been like Jesus in his (Jesus's) death (Phil. 3:10). While this might imply that he was a kind of mystic, living unrealistically with his head in the clouds, he was fully active in the social world.

Paul's legacy consists of his numerous letters, now canonized in the New Testament. They are the product of his total commitment to his mission to bring the whole world, and especially the churches he established, into a readiness for Jesus Christ's expected return to establish God's kingdom.

In Paul we have an example of a Christian focused on a powerful calling that transformed the probability of dying into an insignificant difference between living in this world or living in the next. Dying was certainly real, but he had little opportunity to dwell on it.

Ignatius (?–117 CE): Near the Sword Is Near to God

Ignatius was the third bishop of the church at Antioch (in what is now Syria). He was devoted to maintaining the unity of the church by insisting that the church find its center and focus in the truly and fully human appearance and dying in the flesh of Jesus Christ. In the face of official Roman persecution, he felt that a focus on the unifying power of the crucified and resurrected Christ would not only be truly faithful but also present a powerful posture before the Roman government that had outlawed the new religion. His work found permanent expression in seven letters that he wrote.[6]

The Roman government considered the new Christian religion illegal, but in practice generally adopted a policy of ignoring Christians. This was not so in Ignatius's case. He was arrested, condemned to death, and transported to Rome to face execution by exposure to wild animals. Rather than seeking to avoid this fate, Ignatius embraced it; he would be a martyr.

Martyrs are witnesses; there are many kinds of martyrs—witnesses to or against causes, principles, laws, or persons. Ignatius was not the first Christian martyr, but he is the first one who committed his thoughts on martyrdom to written form. As he traveled to Rome, his concerns were primarily with the churches to which he wrote and with their continuing unity in Christ. His intensified thinking of imminent martyrdom is mentioned very briefly in each of the letters.

What did he think of dying? He expressed his view of dying in peculiar terms. To him, dying meant "achieving" God.[7] By that he meant that he would be with God, in God's presence, and participate fully and immediately in the full communion of God with his creatures. "Near to the sword [death] is near to God"[8] is the way he put it once. Dying would finally make him a true disciple.[9] To achieve this he solicits the prayers and help of his readers[10] with the caveat that they not see their love for him as a reason to help him avoid his martyrdom.[11] He feared that his readers would think that the loving thing to do would be to rescue him or somehow deter him from going through with it. But for him, that would mean not being a disciple and not "achieving" God. He clearly wanted both more than he wanted to escape dying—even the terrible death as the victim of wild animals.[12]

The Christian resources supporting his commitment to faith in the face of the powerful, institutional threat posed by the government include early versions of the creeds and a number of the writings that would be included in the New Testament. Central in his mind was the certainty that Jesus's dying was our resurrection,[13] and that he (Ignatius) had already died through the passion of Jesus[14] so that his death would be a birth.

Ignatius faced the certainty of a horrible dying convinced that it would mean something wonderful for him: completed discipleship and gaining God. He did not feel he could achieve either of those goals in this life outside of the faithful acceptance of martyrdom. His legacy includes two exemplary decisions about his own dying: that he took ownership of his dying, and that he asked his fellow Christians to support him in his martyrdom and not attempt to release him from it.

Julian of Norwich (1342–1416): Christ's Courteous Love

Little detail is known of this English Catholic mystic and hermit who lived much of her life in a cell attached to a church. She has gained fame and popularity through her writings in *Showings*.[15] Her main concern was to find a personal and intense experience of Christ and to share that with others.

What she thought of dying is found in her account of a near death that she experienced when she was thirty years old. During the course of an illness (never described) that lasted several days, she experienced Christ's death pains (i.e., the very pains that Jesus experienced on the cross). She had extensive and detailed visions of Jesus on the cross, in pain, bleeding, shriveling in death. This vision of the dying Christ appeared to her in what she thought would be, and desired to be, her own dying. She concluded that Christ was with her out of his "courteous love" to help her to resist the temptations that attack one's faith at the point of dying.

But she recovered her health and lived another forty-four years, during which she wrote and provided both example and counsel to others who were also seeking an intensely personal faith experience with Christ.

The visions of Jesus for which she fervently longed and prayed constituted the substance of her understanding that Christ was present to those who are dying and that therefore dying was a transition through which Christ courteously and lovingly bore the faithful Christian. Here we have an example of faith finding in Christ a positive helper in the time of dying.

Thomas à Kempis (1380–1471): Blessed Is the Man Who Contemplates Death

Thomas à Kempis was born in Kempen, Germany (thus the "à Kempis"), and he followed his older brother John into a Christian order called the Brothers of the Common Life (founded in 1386). Although the Brothers did not take priestly vows, they lived lives of poverty, chastity, and obedience. They were devoted to a simple life and he lived quietly in the monastery, praying, copying manuscripts, and teaching, never aspiring to high office. He was somewhat mystical and most interested in Christ's sufferings on behalf of humanity.

He did some writing, the most enduring being *The Imitation of Christ*.[16] Among the 107 brief meditations that constitute the work is a section titled "A Meditation upon Death" (book 1, chapter 23). Undoubtedly, more Christians have read about dying from this short meditation than from any other source.

The problem Thomas addresses is that of procrastination. We put off considering dying and what our preparation for it should be. (He had ample time to take his own advice, as he did not die until fifty-three years after the anonymous publication of his book.)

Thomas calmly assesses our situation without threats or scaremongering; everything is offered in a kind but urgent voice. He reminds his readers of the certainty of death and our inability to foretell when it will happen. He also reminds us that we procrastinate not only in preparing for death but even in thinking about it. There is no point in putting off such preparation. We cannot know when it will occur (tomorrow? later today?); we cannot count on a distant "someday" in which we can right our wrongs, repent, and refocus our lives. He points out that if we are now on the wrong track, living longer will only give us more time to dig ourselves deeper into sin; the more time one lives, the more sin it is possible to commit, and the more sins we will have to atone for. It will not be easier later. When one is ill it will be even harder to repent and atone.

One cannot count on friends since we are not really at home in this world. So it is best to contemplate our dying now, rather than put it off. If we start now, in Christ, and live a life of integrity, we will have no fear when the critical moment of dying arrives.

Thomas does not refer specifically to the dying of Jesus or the Christian's death to sin in baptism. Instead he appeals to scriptural admonitions that point out that since we do not know when the critical moment will arrive (Matt. 24:44; 2 Cor. 6:2), we had better utilize what resources we have now in order to ensure our readiness when it does come (Luke 16:9). Thinking that we can get ready to die at a moment's notice is silly. If our lives have been lived in another (non-Christian) fashion, the integrity necessary to face dying as a Christian will not be there.

Thomas was a gentle teacher more than a dramatic example. He reminds us of life's uncertainties and the need to be prepared for the unexpected. He reminds us that living a life of Christian integrity is the best preparation for whatever might come, including dying.

Marguerite Bourgeoys (1620–1700): Take Me Instead

After moving from France to Canada early in life, Marguerite Bourgeoys lived the life of a religious and was formative in developing a religious community that provided education to the indigenous population of the New World. Her commitment was to the success of her mission and she eventually became the head of her order. Life was lived simply, the challenges were great, and her commitment to meet the harsh demands of her calling was complete. In all, hers was a long and exemplary life. Like others in her situation, she spent some time writing devotional and moral guidance for the sisters in her order. Typical was the following: "Think often of death and of the judgment which will follow. Always be ready to appear before God."[17]

Toward the end of 1699, she was ailing and eagerly anticipating union "with her celestial Spouse."[18] Suddenly, a young sister, Catherine, became very ill and as the others surrounded Catherine in what appeared to be her final hour, Marguerite prayed that God would take her, Marguerite, instead. And so it happened. Almost immediately, Catherine improved and Marguerite declined. Though clearly dying, she continued to direct the life of the sisters and finally, twelve days after her prayer request to substitute for Catherine, she lay at death's door. She received the final rites of the faith, the purifying unction and the *viaticum* (Final Communion, which provided spiritual provisions for the trip [*via*] to God).

Marguerite offers an example of what might have been considered an ideal dying throughout most of the time of the church: living a life that would reflect the virtues of the Christian faith, but always with a conscious awareness of death; finally facing dying with courage, even joy; and participating in and drawing comfort from the rites that the church offers to those who are dying. This is not an example only for the spiritually gifted. This was the ideal for all who had lived the Christian faith.

Miguel de Unamuno (1864–1936): I Believe; Help My Unbelief![19]

Miguel de Unamuno is the most modern thinker among this cloud of witnesses. On the surface, he is also the least "religious." He was a Catholic who had a love/hate relationship with the church. He led the quiet life of a college professor, but his political activism enraged his Fascist opponents who were about to plunge Spain into a civil war; they finally placed him under house arrest where he died.

His passion was to find and affirm meaning in life that was threatened by the reality of death. He longed for immortality but reason argued that death was the end of existence. This existential conflict between life and death, reason and passion, head and heart, consumed him in his search for answers to the problem posed by death. He could find no solace to deal with the threat of death, neither from his Catholic religion nor from reasonable philosophical arguments. The church's answers were too neat, too pat, too rational. While his head reasoned death, his heart cried for life.

Since death was the most critical issue humans faced, it was there that the struggle for life must be lost or won. Unamuno was a Christian existentialist who, against all reason and common sense, took a "leap of faith," pinning all of his hopes on Jesus. Nowhere in his voluminous works of poetry, drama, novels, and philosophy is death as clearly faced as it is in a poem he wrote as a kind of commentary or devotional on the dying Christ.[20] His hope was that Jesus's dying might be a dying that promised life in the midst of death. If hope could not be found in Jesus, there could be no other salvation.

While most Christians see the Old Testament as a preparation for the Christ and the New Testament as the report of his coming, Unamuno sees both testaments as understandable only in light of the dying of Jesus. The whole Christian narrative is found in the dying Christ. This is the radical and passionate affirmation of Unamuno (and it is remarkably in tune with Paul's first letter to the Corinthians). If our dying can accomplish anything positive, the test case must be found in Jesus.

So he reflects on the dying Jesus: the cross, the nails, Jesus's forehead, eyes, cheeks, bones, arms, wounds, belly, virility, feet—every detail of the crucifixion. Instead of interpreting this dying through Scripture, Unamuno believes that the dying body of Jesus explains everything else. Unamuno's faith is expressed in these words typical of the underlying hope of the poem: "Death does not hold you; it is you that hold her."[21]

The sheer physical reality of the crucified one leaps from the page as the cross becomes the "kneading trough"[22] in which God made the life-giving bread of the Eucharist.

> Death could not wrench your bones out of their
>   fabric;
> your bones, the tower's stones, and the foundations
> on which rests all Creation. . . .[23]

> And now, in your embrace grasping Death's temple
> with your two arms nailed down onto the
>   cross-beam,
> you pull its pillars down, and as they topple
> at once crush us to death and give us life.[24]

It is clear, after (or within) all the conflict of life and terror of death's threat of nothingness, that Jesus offers hope:

> Thou art the first born of the dead, Thou, ripe
> now for death, art fruit of the tree of life,
> life that never ends, fruit which we must eat
> if we would be free from the second death.
> For Thou hast made of death, that is the end,
> the beginning . . .
> and Thou wast the death of Death at the last![25]

Here we have a modern man, skeptical about religion, individual in his thinking, passionate about life, and with no illusions about death. He leaves us with this challenge: if living is to have meaning, dying must be faced and conquered. If dying is to be conquered, our only alternative is to pin our hopes on Jesus. In Unamuno's view, Jesus lived passionately and died passionately; he was a person whom the church could never fully capture in theology or creed. Yet, ironically, this is also the very Jesus who is at the center of the daily life of the faithful Catholic, dying on the cross and living in the Eucharist. In his understanding of Jesus, Unamuno never moves past the crucifixion to the resurrection; that is another matter.[26] For Unamuno, everything hangs on the cross!

While he might seem unorthodox, here is a very modern person, unconvinced by traditional religion, yet not abandoning the Christian faith for some other spirituality. Perhaps more than anyone else in this cloud of witnesses, Unamuno clings desperately to the dying Jesus.

Dietrich Bonhoeffer (1906–45): Death—the Greatest of Feasts on the Journey to Freedom Eternal[27]

Dietrich Bonhoeffer was a bespectacled, mild-looking German who became convinced that the rise of Hitler in the 1930s would be devastating to the Christian church and to his native country. By the early 1930s he had acquired a teaching position, published, and gained an international reputation as a Christian thinker. In a variety of acts of resistance to the nazification of Germany, and in an effort to strengthen the church against its subversion by the state, Bonhoeffer worked to support a church that would resist being co-opted by Hitler's plans for empire. Friends pleaded with him to sit out the looming war somewhere where he could teach, lecture, and write in peace, but he remained in Germany where, curiously, he took an office job with the *Abwehr*, the German military intelligence agency.

Bonhoeffer's subsequent involvement in a plot to assassinate Hitler resulted from the intersection of two stories: Bonhoeffer's personal narrative as a Christian and that of the German people. Germany had suffered a humiliating defeat in World War I, and by the 1930s, Germans were in the depths of the global financial depression. Adolf Hitler had come into power, riding on aspirations for a glorious revival of a new Germany. Bonhoeffer, by contrast, was a Christian with pacifist ideas who had committed himself to the Christian idea of a community that stood in diametrical opposition to Hitler's vision; it was Hitler's Third Reich versus the kingdom of God.

In 1934, a minority of German Christians affirmed a new confession of faith (the Barmen Declaration) that established that the church could not be controlled by any earthly power or ideology (e.g., the German Nationalist Socialist, or any other political agenda). By the mid-1930s, the fundamental differences between Hitler and the Nazis and Bonhoeffer and others in the new movement of the Confessing Church meant a battle to the end.

There were others in Germany who were uncomfortable with Hitler. Many of the high-ranking military officers in the *Abwehr* were just such persons. When the pain and frustration of many of these persons coalesced into a decision to eliminate Hitler and bring Germany to her senses, Bonhoeffer agreed to help. The alternative would have been to shut his eyes to the self-destruction of his homeland and the slaughter of millions of Jews whom Hitler had blamed for Germany's problems. Even so, for a pacifist like Bonhoeffer, such a decision—to be a party to insurrection and murder—must have been excruciatingly difficult. What may help to explain his commitment to this plot to rid Germany of Hitler was his greater commitment to maintain community, in both Germany and the church, as faithful to God in Christ.

He had thought about the possibility of dying and he was critical of modern views of death. In his *Ethics* he claimed that man had idolized death: "Where death is the last thing, earthly life is all or nothing. Boastful reliance on earthly eternities goes side by side with a frivolous playing with life."[28] But when death is not absolutized and we see that Christ has broken the power of death, we can take of life what it offers and demand no eternities from it.[29]

But the plot to kill Hitler failed, and as the conspiracy unraveled, Bonhoeffer's activities were increasingly limited by the police and he was finally arrested. What he also knew was that he was, like the apostle Paul and Ignatius of Antioch, not only in jail but also in a community of Christians, the (suffering) body of Christ. Christ served others. He was, as Bonhoeffer wrote, "a man for others,"[30] and Bonhoeffer saw each day as an opportunity for him to live Christ's example and to be of service to others who were suffering.

And serve he did. In prison he was the consummate pastor and friend, helping, feeding, and sharing his cigarettes with other prisoners. His one concern was that he would not be strong enough to stand the test of prison and execution. In his imprisonment, he is described by others as radiant, good-tempered, kind, polite, hopeful, grateful, calm, normal, and perfectly at ease; he had become a "man for others," in Christ, dead to himself. He wrote, "We feel that we really belong to death already."[31]

After two years in concentration camps he was finally tried (April 8, 1945) and hanged the following day (only days before the camp was liberated). The camp doctor reported that in his final minute Bonhoeffer was "brave and composed."[32] Despite the final humiliation of being stripped naked, his last act was to kneel and pray under the hangman's noose.

Bonhoeffer wrote more than any other of our small cloud of witnesses. Prior to the war he published much of a formal theological nature. During the war and his imprisonment, his writings were less formal and written against a background of constant dyings. Nearly every letter of his voluminous correspondence from prison mentioned someone who had died in the war. Dying was always near at hand, prompting sermons, lectures, discussions, and the existential questions posed by death.[33] He simply could not avoid communicating openly about dying.

Despite this, Bonhoeffer was certainly not fixated on death. His most powerful legacy is the urgency of his commitment to the body of Christ, the church. "Life in community with God is certainly always directed beyond death."[34] But that life was to be lived in the present: "What would I do if I knew that in four to six weeks it would be all over? That is running through my head. I believe that I would try to teach theology again as before and to preach often."[35] His commitment to maintain a truly Christian community in the face of Nazi perversions of community expressed itself concretely in expressions of love and concern for others, unhindered by the imminence of dying.

He accepted his dying, owned it, and served others in the love of Christ and with the certain hope of the resurrection. His last words were: "This is the end—for me the beginning of life."[36]

Flannery O'Connor (1925–64): Whatever Suits the Lord Suits Me[37]

Flannery O'Connor was an important American author who produced most of her work while suffering what was then (in the 1950s) the incurable and difficult to manage disease of lupus. At fifteen, she had seen her father succumb to the same illness; at twenty-five she was diagnosed with the condition that would sap her physical energies for the next fourteen years.

Despite her affliction, she worked as hard as she could, often only two hours a day, on the writing that was her vocation. While limited physically, she maintained a rich correspondence, much of which survives; it is through her letters that we know of her faith and attitude toward dying.

A disciplined Roman Catholic, she wrote informally and helpfully about Christianity to many of her friends, discussing Catholicism in depth and with great sensitivity to the sensibilities of others. There are virtually no references in her extensive correspondence, however, to her illness and the devastation it had on her. She described herself as "a Catholic peculiarly possessed of the modern consciousness," explaining that "there is nothing harder or less sentimental than Christian realism."[38] In her personal life she appeared quite orthodox, believing what the church teaches, and was regular in devotional reading, prayer, and attendance at Mass.

Once she described her condition as one of "passive diminishment"—a phrase borrowed from the Catholic theologian Teilhard de Chardin. This referred to "those afflictions that you can't get rid of and have to bear. Those that you can get rid of he believes you must bend every effort *to* get rid of."[39] She always appeared more concerned about her writing and her friends than about her physical health.

She reluctantly made a trip to Lourdes, the sanctuary famous for the curative powers attributed to it, but quipped that the only miracle she saw there was that despite all the sick people sharing the waters, no outbreak of an epidemic occurred. She claimed that "sickness before death is a very appropriate thing and I think those who don't have it miss one of God's mercies."[40] She commented on only one book that refers to religious faith and death: the Catholic theologian Karl Rahner's *On the Theology of Death*. "It is great but difficult to read. I read every sentence about three times. . . . I could read it once a year."[41]

As she neared death, she wrote, "The wolf [*lupus* is Latin for wolf], I'm afraid, is inside tearing up the place."[42] She received Final Communion and the Sacrament of the Sick (Extreme Unction) shortly before dying on August 3, 1964. Flannery O'Connor offers an example of someone who led a life severely limited to a few hours of vitality each day, all of which she filled with productive work. Her relationships were other-centered; her energies, directed at her work. All of this was done within the discipline of a conventional religious piety, which was not contorted by nor wasted on concern for her terminal condition.

Penny Lernoux (1940–89): Learning the Ultimate Powerlessness of Christ

Penny Lernoux worked as a photojournalist for major American magazines, was married, and had a daughter. She was a Catholic—at first distanced from the church, then brought close through her experiences with the Christian poor in the third world. She died one month after being diagnosed with lung cancer.

In the course of her work, she was faced with the injustices suffered by the poor in Latin America. She came to believe that Christians in the first world were complicit in the institutionalization of the terror, repression, poverty, and hopelessness suffered by millions in the poorest parts of the world. Her mission in life was telling the story of the oppressed poor of Latin America—in pictures, articles, and several books. Blocking that mission was the institutionalization of violence against the poor by governments and even by the church's conservative hierarchy.

What gave her courage to continue her work even as she was dying was her experience of being with the poor, seeing Christ in the poor, and knowing him as essentially one of the poor. In his work, Jesus was poor and in his dying he was without anything. When we are truly with him we are also poor and so we come to dying. The solidarity with Christ and with the poor in their struggle provided the faith that transcended death.

What supported Lernoux in that belief was the face of the Catholic Church that had recently begun to turn toward the poor. It was a new era for Catholicism with the celebration of Vatican II, an epic council of the Catholic Church in the 1960s, and, more specifically and more important, councils of more liberal-thinking bishops in Medellín, Colombia, in 1968, and Puebla, Mexico, in 1979. In those councils, the church spoke of a Christ for the poor and committed itself to be more sensitive to their condition. Lernoux took that commitment seriously and was able to live and die in that mission.

Her professional legacy was that of publications bringing the inequities suffered by weaker neighbors to the attention of a rich American public.[43] Personally, her growth as a Christian culminated in learning her own powerlessness, which she described as a cleansing experience, in the ultimate powerlessness of Christ.[44]

Joseph Cardinal Bernardin (1928–96): A Priest First, a Patient Second[45]

Joseph Cardinal Bernardin began his preparation for the priesthood at age seventeen. Early in his priesthood he committed himself to a devotional discipline of emptying himself in prayer in order to let God into his life. This was a lifelong practice but also one of constant challenge. His devotion to his congregants was full-time, and he later realized that it had often been easy to substitute "good works" for the more private and disciplined life of prayer and the "letting go" that he believed could empty himself of himself and open him to Jesus Christ.

Ordained a priest in 1952, he rose rapidly through the Catholic hierarchy, first as auxiliary bishop (1966), then archbishop (1972), and finally cardinal (1982). He served the two million Catholics of the Chicago area as archbishop until pancreatic cancer ended his life. A first brush with pancreatic cancer (1995) was aggressively treated, and he continued his leadership in the Archdiocese of Chicago as well as in numerous national and international obligations that earned him much well-deserved appreciation. The cancer returned (1996) and was inoperable. It was then that he added a personal ministry to other cancer patients to his workload. By the time of his death, the list of cancer victims for whom he was praying exceeded seven hundred.

His primary obligations, however, continued to be his parishioners in the Archdiocese of Chicago. He saw himself first and foremost as their priest and only secondarily as a cancer patient. He still worked at the discipline of self-emptying so that Christ could take over his life completely; he saw his cancer as a gift to help him maintain that commitment. In his memoir, it is clear that Christ is central in his mind as he considers his vocation (as shepherd),[46] the loneliness of sickness and pain (Jesus in Gethsemane),[47] and the yoke of pain that Christ promises to bear with us.[48] In addition to the short book chronicling the intimate and personal side of his illness, he took the unusual step of revealing publicly much of the details of his illness through press conferences.[49] "Throughout my own illness I have shared the news about my health as it has been made known to me. My family are the people of metropolitan Chicago. . . . And my family has a right to know how I am doing."[50]

He concludes his personal reflections with the affirmation that he was able "to look upon death as a friend, not an enemy"[51] and that he faced dying with peace and the conviction that he would be at home with God.

Like the examples of others in this chapter, the final weeks of Bernardin's life were filled with the kinds of works that had always characterized his vocation: caring for his flock. There is more. Bernardin claims that his illness helped him to empty himself of himself, of his future, of everything that would keep him from serving Christ in the moment and from everything that would prevent him from accepting death. And he communicated fully, with his doctors (and they with him), and with his parishioners—all 2.3 million of them.

In her summary of Bernardin's end of life, Therese Lysaught points to four noteworthy aspects of his story that may provide a map for others:[52] he allowed his dying to be public (known to his constituency), he enlarged his earlier already expansive ministry to encompass cancer sufferers, he came to regard death "not as an enemy but as a friend,"[53] and the experience of dying opened for him a deeper understanding of the power of the Christian sacraments.

Surrounded by So Great a Cloud of Witnesses

All who are in Christ will die in Christ. They are of the community of the faithful awaiting entry to the community of those who died faithfully. Yet no one knows "how to" die. These ten witnesses have bequeathed us their thoughts— some in detail, others more allusively—on their own dying. These thoughts constitute a treasury of resources on which we might draw should they seem appropriate.

Each of the witnesses was able to access different resources from that larger treasury of experience, tradition, community, art, philosophy, Scripture, communal or mystical experience, and even official church pronouncements and liturgical practices. These responses occur over two millennia, in widely separated parts of the world and under widely different circumstances. They are not only important in and of themselves, but they tell us that among the multitude of those who have died faithfully without having left a written record of their thoughts, there have been many who had thought through helpful ways to face their own dying. So we can be encouraged: there are resources upon which to draw and there is a broad canvas upon which we can each faithfully and helpfully paint our own vision of the end of life.

Discussion Questions

1. Tell the story of the dying of someone—a loved one, someone you read about, or anyone else.
2. Which of the characters in this chapter can you most identify with? Why?
3. Which of the Christian resources you know of seems to offer the best support for facing dying?
4. Can you tell a story of how you might want to face dying?

8

A Good Dying

Can we possibly imagine a good dying?[1] We would need to talk about it. We have seen that a closed awareness to dying not only doesn't work, but includes side effects for everyone involved, including congregations and pastors (chapter 1). We have seen how the church evades both the reality of dying and the opportunities to do ministry if dying is outsourced to secular providers by the church (chapter 2). But we have also been reminded that Jesus Christ is the Lord of the Dying and as such knows what it means to suffer even the most cruelly painful dying; he also promises something unfathomably hopeful after that death (chapter 3). Having such a Savior makes Christians a people who have already died to sin, to self, and to the world's way of doing things; we know that we are equipped to cope with dying in ways that are not embraced by culture, health care, and other structures heavily valued in times of serious and terminal illness (chapter 4). One of the main resources we are given is the gift of communication: the creation of shared meaning; the Lordship and example of Jesus Christ, the Word of God; and Jesus's sanctification of language that provides content and means to lovingly and helpfully care for the ill and the carers of the ill (chapter 5). We acknowledge publicly an active concern for the dying and entertain the possibilities of a good dying for those afflicted with a terminal diagnosis (chapter 6). And we have heard accounts of Christians who have drawn on these resources in uniquely personal, creative, and exemplary ways to face their own dying (chapter 7).

It is time to face *the* question: Can all of these gifts come together to make possible what we might consider a good dying? The previous chapters have been reminders of what we already have available, but all too often we have not taken advantage of them. In this chapter we shall bring those Christian resources together with constructive means of communicating among those involved in terminal illness situations to suggest how opportunities might be created to help each dying person die well.

We are aware of how overreaching it must sound to make a claim providing the "how tos" of a good dying. There is the danger of sounding as though we have collected all the suggestions from the entire history of the church and are saying, "Here is the recipe for the good dying." We apologize if we sound that way. No one can assure another of "success" in the matter of dying. What we can do is bring to mind what we as a Christian church have received from Christ and attempted in our efforts to live faithfully. And so it is with humility that we proceed.

It is foundational in the Christian experience that nothing can separate us from the love of God. In the passage where this claim is made (Rom. 8:38–39), the first thing that will not be able to separate us from God's love is death. In a variation on the same theme, Paul writes elsewhere that "to live is Christ and to die is gain" (Phil. 1:21 NIV). We believe that "all things work together for good for those who love God" (Rom. 8:28). What is difficult is to find that good in facing dying. We know from Jesus Christ that dying is not the ultimate problem to be addressed (and solved) with our lives. Our ultimate challenge or test (opportunity) of faith is our relationship with God. That is the relationship that governs all others, including our relationship with ourselves, which is where dying enters the picture. Drawing on considerations of a "good death," let us consider what might constitute it and how the Christian faith can offer the richest possibility for fulfilling the needs of the dying.[2]

Criteria for Good Dying

There is no one set of generally agreed-upon criteria for a good dying. Those seeking to find it seem free to offer their own list or to adopt the suggestions of others. Some "lists" are clearly religious, either with a generally spiritual or specifically Christian orientation. Others are noticeably secular, with no (or virtually no) religious dimension.[3] Additionally, the focus of these good death lists is indeed on the death. We must extend the journey to death in these criteria and frame this as a good *dying*, recognizing it as a process rather than an arrived-at end point. All that said, the following definition, taken from a study summarizing four major Christian writers, may be instructive:

> A "good death" will be one where the person receives the mercy of God, possesses a lively hope of enjoying eternal life with Christ and with all the saints, and surrenders his or her life to God praying "Lord Jesus, receive my spirit" (Acts 7:59). The traditional picture of a good death is one where the person is aware up to the very end, in which reconciliation to God and to one's brothers and sisters is explicit and sacramental, and in which the acceptance of death is conscious and peaceful.[4]

These criteria are helpful, but need to be woven together with concerns for the physical realities of a terminal illness that most frequently include delirium, confusion, lack of consciousness, and pain.[5] Keeping our specifically Christian summary in mind, then, we turn to health-related issues— understood in the broadest terms—that can contribute to a good dying.

Pain and Symptom Management

There seems to be a broad spectrum along which different people experience pain. Most of us have experienced or witnessed a variety of pain/discomfort, and have had at least one loved one who has experienced dying that drags on painfully; no one wants such a dying. Fortunately, palliating pharmaceuticals and therapies continue to improve the management of pain and symptoms. Without any cynicism, it must be noted that the attention that health-care professionals pay to physical suffering is central to their work. The technical, chemical, and biological resources afforded by the developments in health care are appropriate and needed in the process of dying.

Historically, Christians have had a generally positive relationship with health professionals, and nursing and medicine have grown as successful sciences largely within the ideological framework of hospitals created by the church.[6]

But pain and symptom management is not the only problem to address if we are to secure the possibility of a good dying. The Christian faith thanks God for the knowledge, skills, and availability of health care. What it does not accept is the idea that such care is all that we need at the end of life.

The church cannot sit on the sidelines and hope to be invited to minister. We have noted the solid foundation established in Jesus the Word upon which to begin communicating about dying and with the dying, and with those who minister medically. Perhaps the beginnings of good dying will be found in the church initiating dialogue not only within its fellowship, and with its ailing brothers and sisters, but also with health-care providers. And we dare not forget the promise of Jesus from the Sermon on the Mount: "Blessed are you who weep now, for you will laugh" (Luke 6:21b).

Clear Goals of Care

The goal of care at the end of life is a relatively recent, good news/bad news topic. Advancements in health-care technology and practice have made it possible for people with certain problems to be "saved" for a time from dying. That is the good news.

The bad news is that these same techniques can physically prolong the life of the body in ways that ignore or eliminate other, nonphysical dimensions of life. Being "attached to a machine" may mean continued life, but being part of a machine rather than an independently functioning and self-directed individual may not be one's idea of really living. For example, being sustained physically with a feeding tube might be unacceptable for many who did not realize the commitment they were making when they decided to allow the employment of life-extending treatments. So death may be preferred to a life that is merely a function of effective but limiting technology. Open communication among all stakeholders is important in terms of understanding the limitations of extreme health interventions or curative therapies no longer effective on dying individuals, and talking through what a dying person really wants to experience at the end of life.

What is a futile health intervention? In the world of health care, if two medical providers agree that an intervention will cause harm and no gain, it is deemed futile. Still, some families demand symbolic interventions—therapies that have the potential to cause increased pain and ensure extreme financial costs in the final days of life.[7] Many patients have not discussed their end-of-life care with family, and once near the end of life lack the consciousness and clarity to do so. More and more is being discovered about the impact of terminal illness and health interventions on patients' caregivers; disturbing rates of post-traumatic stress disorder (PTSD), anxiety, stress, and depression have been scientifically proven for this population.[8] Research in the last two decades has also established that physicians who have lower communication skills in discussing end-of-life realities intervene at a higher rate.[9] Patient fear of clinician abandonment plays a larger and larger role in splintered specialized care. Often, patients or families fear they will be left by their clinician and "dumped" on hospice, thus motivating extreme efforts at curative treatments too near the end of life.[10] To complicate matters, religious coping has been found to correlate strongly with extreme end-of-life interventions deemed futile.[11] Ours is a non-exhaustive list identifying some factors that compel Americans to die in pain, with the highest expense, and away from home.

There are ethical issues that are complex and urgent but that seldom arise in the immediacy of an individual illness.[12] So the church may need to clutter the process of working out the definition of "futile" by introducing concerns that might otherwise have been omitted, for example, by asking, what is the most faithful use of resources under consideration? But at the more immediate and urgent level, the church's responsibility is to focus on issues of love, forgiveness, and hope. Human life is good, sacred, and valued; it is not, finally, ultimate. Clinical interventions that disregard a patient's real goals of care and the needs of his or her caregivers begin to appear extreme. Christian faith has the burden of placing life in a context in which each one is valued, not a context in which one is valued at a cost to others. At the heart of that context is the story of creation: Adam and Eve were created good and did not need anything more or different from what they had. How different we all might have been if we had heeded the beatitude implied in Genesis 3: "Blessed are you when you are content with who you are and what you have."

Family

Family is important and may be defined in a variety of ways. In American culture, the family can include nuclear family members, usually with some elasticity that might embrace grandparents, in-laws, and other relatives. Family could also be a partner, close friend(s) ("like a 'brother' to me"), or, finally, and in essentially biblical terms, the church. Whoever is part of a sick person's family also faces suffering of a reciprocal nature. This family is the second-order patient. Most people seem to want to die surrounded (physically or emotionally, or both) by their intricately knitted group, the assumption and hope being that this will provide the best source of emotional support and bulwark against fear of abandonment. Sometimes, achieving that support can be problematic.

While respecting the dying person's personal and operative definition of family, as well as caregiver definitions of family, the community's self-understanding of its own function as larger family is something it can navigate without demanding engagement from the dying person or her or his family. The church should ask: Are we self-consciously "family" in the biblical sense? Do we see ourselves as a family of aliens, traveling through life as exiles and sympathetic to all whose experience, such as dying, seems alien? In what concrete ways can we be family to the dying?

Illustrative in this respect is the history of the ways in which Christians have practiced the ministry of what Paul Ramsey calls "only caring,"[13] which is seen in Scripture in the practice of visiting and anointing the sick (James 5:14), in monastic developments formalized in the *Rule of St. Benedict*, and in maintaining a communal approach to care of the dying. We are reminded of Ramsey's comment that "the sting of dying is solitude."[14]

The story of the church includes the birth of the hospital. While Christians cannot claim a unique relationship with the concept of the hospital, religions have frequently been the source of care for the dying. Being with the dying was often all that anyone could do, so the notion of hospital (or hospital-ity) was an appropriate way to view this ministry to sisters and brothers who approached death. Today the church needs to assert its "family-ness" and its "hospital-ity" in the face of the medicalizing isolation of the sorry fact that many people die in a medical setting and die without ready access to the people and place that provide the most comfort.[15] Neither is a fate that God wants for his creatures. Let us remember the blessing from the psalmist who wrote, "How very good and pleasant it is when kindred live together in unity! . . . For there the LORD ordained his blessing, life forevermore" (Ps. 133:1, 3b).

Living the Best Life

Knowing that someone has lived well and is dying with the same character and integrity with which she or he faced other moments of difficulty is something that can contribute to a good dying. That a Christian would embody Christian virtues or practices throughout *all* of life is desirable for seeking a good dying. Instead of employing culturally approved "virtues" (e.g., defiance, black humor, self-absorption, "beating the illness"), the Christian virtues of kindness, love, and patience,[16] while difficult to maintain in situations of pain and frustration, are preferable. This is so because a Christian wants to care for those who are caring for her or him. For example, accepting help is not generally considered a secular virtue by the independent-minded person. But accepting and receiving help from those loved ones whose primary concern is helping the dying is one of the few concrete actions that a person otherwise incapacitated by weakness and pain can actually do.[17]

But things fall apart; in dying, a person's story and body are in uncharted territory. A personal narrative is challenged and may be in chaos; the body no longer responds or functions.

"Things fall apart; the center cannot hold."[18] That is another way to describe sin: a falling apart so that the center, God, is left out. In ordinary times, we subdivide our lives into segments. The personal part can be different from the public part. The family part can be separated from the job part. The Sunday Christian part can be held away from the Monday secular part. When we are well, we are not disturbed by this fragmentation. But when everything is falling apart and there seems no solid center to hold on to or nothing to hold things together, that is when faith can feel threatened. Through everything, however, God's promise is to continue faithful. But still, we may refocus our faith; that is what happens when we outsource the care and understanding of the dying and fully entrust their well-being to others. We are living dangerously. We are finally outsourcing our faith, trusting in the advice that comes to us from American secular culture and blocking out all others in desperate attempts to avoid the inevitable.

Instead, faith can be our support and guide even in these moments when hope can be threatened. Little has been said thus far about *faith*, a word much too easily tossed about. However, in dying, faith can come into play in a way unparalleled in any other aspect of life. It will certainly be one of the few alternatives left to a dying person.

We are given the promise that what has happened through Christ for the dying is that sin, death's sting, is removed; and we can accept that promise. The power of sin is what could turn us from God should we turn and rely upon our own resources; but it was shown to be powerless in any relationship with God in the life, dying, and rising of Jesus Christ. So in faith terms, in our theology of dying, dying is revealed as something of the emperor's new clothes: a boogeyman with no power over those who trust in God through Christ.

Faith is what Jesus Christ has given us: an offer of contact with our creator, a means of being extricated from the difficulties into which we have gotten but from which we see no escape. In that faith that Jesus lived and shared, we have resources to deal with dying as he dealt with dying.

The Christian story on display throughout these pages constitutes a claim that Christians embrace as applicable to themselves. The person who faithfully accepts and lives in those Christian claims and assertions has a story that holds him or her together and provides a place to live and to die. What is the reality to which such faith points? It is that in our dying with Christ in baptism, and our being fed by him in the Eucharist, that we have already been living a new life, open to the gifts that God gives. The physical death that threatened those gifts no longer threatens or terrifies. In an odd way, Christians control death, we "own" it (1 Cor. 3:21–23) and instead of being in fear or bondage to it, we have been freed from its terror (Heb. 2:14).

The author of Hebrews offers a definition of faith; it is "the assurance of things hoped for, the conviction of things not seen" (Heb. 11:1). The dying Christian cannot see ahead to the work of dying or beyond that to death and beyond death. In dying, faith is the conviction that God will care for us as we embark on this unique experience.

Dying has been experienced by many, each differently and in uniquely personal ways; the death (and beyond) toward which dying moves us is utterly unknown. We might like to know and to ask as many did on several occasions, "Where are you going?" (John 7:35; 13:36; 14:5). We might ask, "What will it be like?" "How is the getting there?" Rather than provide guidance, Jesus gives the answer that was implicit from the beginning (i.e., our baptism): "I am the way. . . . No one comes . . . except through me" (John 14:6). Even Jesus, who returned to his friends after experiencing death, did not provide a road map of the way or a description of the destination. The wisest thing seems to be to accept our ignorance of what lies ahead and to admit that we cannot know. It is unknown. To the extent that it is known, it is known to God.

172

Is that not enough? What do we need to know in order to face dying, death, and beyond? We have the assurance of Jesus, who died and rose and who invites us to die and rise with him in baptism and become his own. We have Jesus, who was killed but raised to new life, and who invites us to bring our brokenness to him in confession as we partake of the Eucharist and then experience his feeding us in our new life with his own body/blood broken and spilled for us into new life. We have Jesus's assurance that he is the Way. Are these promises, which we have accepted throughout our lives as Christians and members of the body of Christ, not enough to assure us that when we face the unknowns of dying and death that God will be there for us as God was there for Jesus? Faith is the quintessential descriptor of the attitude, posture, and mind-set for us as we face the unknowns of dying and death. Faith is a curious act, which consists of our action, but is not action on our part. Our part is submission to forces beyond our control. Trying to take control is ultimately folly and sinful. It is folly because it can't work. It is sinful because it is one more separation from God. As one author suggests, dying is "active consummation of the self from within and passive submission to destruction from without."[19]

While God may appear (or not appear at all) to be distant, the one concrete "hook" the dying person has on which to hang all hope is Jesus Christ, who himself died and has invited us into his life through his dying. The Christian has already accepted this invitation. The Christian's dying is the quintessential moment of faith. It is the moment before the cross, to which we bring nothing and in which we face the Christ who has nothing, and we both have nothing in which to hope except God.

But curiously, this is a faith act, which we actually perform ourselves; it is a choice we make that no other can make for us. It is the leap of faith that indeed is made in the face of the great unknown of death. It is the final and climactic moment of our (physical) lives.

We accept dying as an act of faith or we do not accept it in faith. Accepting dying in faith means entrusting ourselves to God with no preconditions or demands. Since we are ignorant of what is to come, we can be cognizant of the God to whom we entrust ourselves because we do know that God's love is greater than the power of dying and death.

And while it may sound harsh, "dying persons have a responsibility to die in a manner that has contributed to the good of the community that has nurtured them."[20] Those who are not dying want to give to as well as receive from the dying person, who has so much to contribute. The church may need to consider this "pedagogy of suffering" that the terminally ill can offer. Even at the end of life, a blessing can be conferred as Scripture reports the voice from heaven saying, "Blessed are the dead who from now on die in the Lord" (Rev. 14:13).

Finishing Unfinished Business

A terminal diagnosis never comes at the right time. Our bucket lists get longer and longer. There are always too many tasks to complete, too many obligations still to be met. The dying person is not only running out of time, but out of strength, the ability to concentrate, even clarity of thought. How can life's to-do list be managed in the face of death? How can the dying do much of anything? They would seem to be the weakest and least healthy for any tasks. The frustrations of not finishing can be one more burden draining the energies of a dying patient. That same frustration can wear on caregivers as they may not be able to complete tasks either.

Perhaps a different understanding of health is required. Christian nurses, writing on the care of the dying, employ a definition of health that sees it (health) as optimum realization of all the possibilities for an organism (physical or social) at any given moment in its life.[21] An organism fatally compromised by trauma or disease still can realize whatever limited possibilities are still available. If unfinished business cannot be finished, perhaps the ill person can forgive herself or himself for not finishing. The finishing of unfinished business, or adjusting to its impossibility, may also clear the way for what one writer called "directionality"—the change of focus on the part of one dying away from what cannot be finished toward what will come next, a looking positively toward the future.[22]

The dying person is someone who is valuable within the community and her or his frustrations can be opportunities for the church to find concrete ways in which to express what might otherwise be its own overwhelming frustration in its human inability to stave off dying. It is justifiable to expect that the dying have something to contribute. We can covenant, each to do our own part in getting things done.

God's promise to us all is expressed in the beatitude "Blessed is that slave whom his master will find at work when he arrives" (Matt. 24:46). The blessing is not contingent upon work completed, but about the worker's commitment to the master.

Addressing Conflicts

At its core, the Christian faith has a God who forgives and hopes that those who are forgiven will in turn forgive. It is worth noting that the only thing we promise in the Lord's Prayer is to forgive: "Forgive us our debts, as we also have forgiven our debtors" (Matt. 6:12). Serious, open communication will be necessary. Without it, matters that need resolution may not surface, or, if they do, may not be resolved. No one should be deprived of resolving unsettled issues for lack of the right words. Death can seem to be a stop sign before which we bring things safely to a halt. Ruptures in relationships can be nurtured; conflicts addressed; guilt absolved. Forgiveness can be either given or received, or both. The period of dying can be a time of coming together instead of coming apart. We can be free to die or to let our loved ones die.

Conflicts may come in as many forms as there are relationships: long-standing ones, the origins of which may have long been forgotten; others more recent; some deep and complex; others caused by simple misunderstandings and easily remedied. Loved ones may not want the dying person to die. They may express that hope openly, even persistently. An unintended consequence may be that the dying person then feels guilty for dying! Reconciliation with the clinicians who cannot keep a person from dying despite all of their best efforts may need to be added to the list of conflicts to be addressed. The cost of unresolved guilt, anger, disputes, and conflict at dying and death is complicated grief for the living. Additionally, a lack of social support (i.e., church community) is a primary indicator of complicated grief and bereavement.[23]

As we saw in chapter 1, conflicts that are not addressed before death may haunt the church for years. There may be no criterion for a good dying that may have more impact on the community than that of resolving conflicts and offering and receiving forgiveness. God's promise is found in the words Jesus offered in the Sermon on the Mount: "Blessed are the peacemakers, for they will be called children of God" (Matt. 5:9).

Answers to Existential and Spiritual Questions

There are different kinds of questions. There are questions that cannot be answered with clarity and assurance. "Why has this happened to me?" may be in that category. But just because we don't know the answer doesn't mean that it doesn't deserve a serious response.[24]

Then there are the questions that Christians have special answers for: What is the meaning of life? What, where, and how will I be after I die? Have I made the best of my life? Will I see my loved ones again? These are the questions that may not have precisely detailed answers, but Scripture assures us that the answers will come from a caring creator God.

Then there are the anxieties and worries we bring in the form of secrets, guilt, remorse, regret, depression, anger, and blame. These are real and Christians cannot simply deal with them in the modern secular fashion as mere "emotional hang-ups"[25] to be treated with more pharmaceuticals or therapy. Sometimes modern psychology interprets these feelings as fear of oblivion or loss of identity.[26] But even the best modern techniques of sympathetic listening and therapy cannot always deliver the dying from what Christians know as sin or guilt. This may be one of the most difficult questions; Jesus asked it: "My God, my God, why have you forsaken me?" (Mark 15:34). That question could be prompted by pain, or it could be a lament that sin was overpowering the loving power of God and separating the dying from God's care.

In previous epochs, sin and guilt faced every dying person; and, one way or another, they dealt with it. The reason sin is the Christian's problem is that sin is what has separated the dying creature from the eternal creator; the crucial question is whether that separation will continue. What gives sin its power, perhaps its last chance to triumph and make dying a total (eternal, ontological, spiritual) catastrophe, is the idea that Paul (and Jesus) battled throughout the Scriptures: that humans have made their own laws (ethical, religious, ritual, communal, or political) for determining our relationship with God. But we are not in charge of what can assure our relationship with God. We know that Christ has already established that relationship. We cannot break it; we can only deny and reject it. Christians understand that the law does not carry that burden or power. Instead God has "give[n] us the victory through our Lord Jesus Christ" (1 Cor. 15:57). It is despair, not dying, that is the worst thing.[27]

God has promised a blessing, even for those who may search and long for answers when Jesus promised, "Blessed are those who hunger and thirst for righteousness, for they will be filled" (Matt. 5:6).

Peace and Acceptance

Finding calm in the midst of the chaotic and painful work of dying may be extremely difficult. But it might be a bit easier if the needs expressed in the previous sections are at least somewhat addressed.

Peace (read: stability) is always challenged, or threatened, by change. The change experienced by the birth of a new member of the group is dramatic and substantial, but usually greeted joyfully. Parents may be stunned by new responsibilities, older siblings threatened with jealousy by an additional love object, first-time grandparents weighed down by the reality of time passing and years accumulating. But birth is a change to which adaptation can be enthusiastic.

Change threatened by dying—a wife becomes a widow, a child becomes an orphan—is not welcome; seldom is it foreseen; less often are preparations made. The challenge to the church is to maintain the bond of peace in the face of changes. While some changes are good and others threatening, the church, in Christ, can take a relatively objective perspective, always ready to dampen undue enthusiasm (introduce realism) and shore up broken spirits. How can we find contentment in the midst of flux and change? Perhaps this can be pursued with a biblical understanding of peace in mind. Peace (*shalom* in the original Hebrew of Scripture) meant a kind of harmonious inclusion of all things in a complete whole. A dying that met these criteria would be a part of peace, wholeness, a good dying. For examples of this peace, see Genesis 15:15: "You [Abram] shall go to your ancestors in peace; you shall be buried in a good old age"; and 2 Kings 22:20b: "And you shall be gathered to your grave in peace." Jeremiah prophesies that even an enemy of Israel "shall not die by the sword; you shall die in peace" (Jer. 34:4c–5a). In Job 21:13, Job complains that even the unjust can experience *shalom*: "They spend their days in prosperity, and in peace they go down to Sheol." This peace is not found only in the attitudes of humans, but includes the complex of relationships that constitute the environment in which humans live. In Job 5:23, Job's friend Elisha assures him of a future good outcome from his sufferings in which even nature participates in the promised *shalom*: "For you shall be in league with the stones of the field, and the wild animals shall be at peace with you."

Each of the twenty-one letters found in the New Testament was written to a reader (or community of readers) about a problem (or several) that was troubling and even dividing the community. Of the twenty-one letters, eighteen wish the reader(s) "peace" in the greeting or closing. The love of God in Christ made everything okay. Everything? According to Paul, nothing can separate us from the love of God (Rom. 8:38–39), "to live is Christ and to die is gain" (Phil. 1:21 NIV), and "I can do all things through him [Christ]" (Phil. 4:13). Remember, this is not just Paul saying this; the whole church accepted his understanding of the Christian life in the process of the canonization of the New Testament. The Spanish Catholic Miguel Unamuno, who struggled mightily with the terrible finality of dying and the hope for life beyond death, captured this possibility in the title of one of his novels, *Peace in War*.

The promise of the Christian gospel is that there is peace available in the direst circumstances. Whether we can be assured that any of our dying sisters and brothers will buy into that notion and find the promised peace is not certain. What we can assure, however, is that we, the church, affirm the reality and availability of that peace in the way we conduct our individual and communal, familial lives in the church.

The Christian call to "only caring"[28] rather than pursuing every means to prolong life may seem frustratingly inadequate, but it can be a form of peacefulness. Instead of seeking one more opinion, one more medication, one more experimental procedure, "only caring" may be the most therapeutic (non)response that can facilitate a final peace and acceptance on the part of all participants. We are out of practice at "only caring," as we have come to a point in

Western culture in which caring is enacted through busy caretaking. This consists primarily of engaging in the health-care enterprise of the West, in which the majority of caregiving time goes into driving, cleaning, physical labor, medical care, clinical appointments, and treatment.[29] "Only caring" can be a rich and positive approach to which we turn in spelling out a ministry of relating to and speaking with the dying in ways that can make possible the promise from Christ, "Blessed are the peacemakers, for they will be called children of God" (Matt. 5:9).

We do not turn to "only caring" because we cannot think of anything else. In fact, we always hold in mind the promises of Scripture: our hope is secure, not because we hope harder than others hope, but because, as Paul writes in Colossians 1:5, our "hope [is] laid up for you in heaven." It is established and secured by God. In the same way we are assured in more spectacular terms that "in fact Christ has been raised from the dead, the first fruits of those who have died . . . so all will be made alive in Christ" (1 Cor. 15:20–22). Both the "only caring" and the "only cared for" share equally in the hope and assurance of God's care before, during, and after death.

Using Our Gifts for Ministry

We conclude by inviting the reader to imagine a ministry of communicating with and about the dying that can open us to those blessings promised in Christ. We know that when the journey of dying has begun in earnest, everything changes. Issues of health and medicine are taken more seriously, and patients and their caregivers commit themselves to the most extraordinary measures of care by the medical establishment. Later in the disease process, when dying becomes an active process of dwindling and reduced activity, involved Christians, and by implication, the church, reach a crossroads. What can the church do that was not done at the clinic?

What can a fellow Christian offer as an improvement over the ministrations of a caring nurse? Is there a positive path in this wilderness that we have not noticed in our haste to seek a medical cure to a huge human problem?

One option is to adopt the culturally approved model of silence, denial, and avoidance. The other is to confess openly, "We've been there, we've done that; this is where we belong: together at the foot of the cross." Both options are in their own way "religious." The first admits to a faith decision that prefers a journey of secular health-care treatment that might (if we are lucky) include some psychosocial care. The second is a leap of faith, a response of a broader scope.

A few rare saints of the church are able to do that and serve both the dying and themselves (when they die) faithfully and well. The rest of us may need some help, some prompting, some resources, and some tested strategies. We will all benefit from an enhanced grasp of a Christian theology of dying, a more insightful understanding of the sinful but attractive alternative responses available in popular secular culture, and a set of clear and appropriate guidelines for end-of-life communication.

What can we learn from communication scholars about concrete ways in which the church can seek to communicate effectively in addressing end-of-life issues? Their goal is to translate the most effective learning tools into everyday life situations in order to improve the lives of those in need. What follows is a simple acronym, TABLE, that may be helpful in combining biblical and christological insights (theology of dying) with communication strategies into a useful tool for the church. It uses the central Christian practice of gathering at Christ's Table to celebrate and receive the Eucharist, to commune with others, and to celebrate the death and resurrection of Jesus Christ. That seems a fitting place to gather and frame the community's verbal and nonverbal communication on dying. Instead of abandoning ourselves to another secular scheme, our existence is rooted in a Christology of the Word.

Invitation to the TABLE

Acronyms[30] can sometimes be helpful mnemonic devices to help us remember the elements of something; occasionally the acronyms themselves point to an important dimension of the whole. In this case, the term "table" serves both as an acronym for elements or aspects of a strategy as well as a metaphor—indeed more than a metaphor—for the central powerful narrative of our faith: the Eucharist. It is Jesus Christ who invites us to the table: his Table. It is that Lord whom we celebrate at the eucharistic table and our conviction is that as long as we are gathered at that table and focused on that Christ, our ministry to the dying will go forth to all as a more comprehensive alternative to anything available elsewhere.

This table of suggestions for communication is not simply good practical theology (i.e., how Christians should behave faithfully with and for others), but the result of evidence-based research on end-of-life communication developed by researchers seeking a better dying for all.[31] This is not a guaranteed "do-it-yourself" guide to success in facilitating a good death. This is not an exhaustive or five-step program. It is offered as a closing reminder that Christ himself invites us to where the needs of the dying can be met in ways that provide greater fulfillment than health care and a secular end-of-life model alone can offer.

T *Is for Talk*

Talk, a central vehicle to shared meaning, is what is needed. An ongoing circle of encoding, interpreting, and decoding meaning is the partner to talk and achieves understanding for those engaged in the experience. The talk to which we are invited and to which we contribute is rooted in a Christology of the Word. Because Jesus is the Word and because he has been given to us by God, our words can be as transparent and bold as his.

The world today is a place of constant chatter: the media buries us in talk; and politicians, celebrities, advertisers, sports heroes, and announcers talk in verbiage that is more hype than fact. The dying person lives in a world where the prevailing language may sound like that of the biblical Babel in its pretensions of attaining the unreachable. A patient's process of listening is often overwhelmed in the crossfire of language, while achieving little shared meaning.

So the church invites the dying person and gathers itself at the table for talk and deep listening. This is not the examination table of the clinic or hospital. It is more like the kitchen table with its informality and warmth where conversation flows freely and issues are dealt with openly. It is also like the Communion Table where Christ is present and ready to feed us from his own suffering and strength.

The dying person who has come from the hospital or clinic, from the examination room or the treatment facility, from the lab or the pharmacy, has come from a world in which a particular story has been assumed, believed, told, and retold. The story is something like this: "We know what ails you and we have ways to 'treat' you." The secular, medical language is narrow, focused on physical repair, and not only does not expand to embrace other, collateral issues but also leaves the patient as a bit player in another's (the clinician's) story. The patient may actually have very little grasp of the medical, scientific, and health-care narrative into which clinicians have placed him or her.

The churches and pastors of chapter 1 did not talk, did not gather at the table. They seem to have gone through their church obligations and routines unaware that help was at hand. We heard nothing of the prayers of lament, the words of complaint lifted to God, nor did we hear of the desperate prayers for miracle healings.[32] Indeed, individuals and the church need always to pray, to talk to God about the situation, whether in anger, in desperation, in resignation, or in peace. This is part of the connectedness that the dying Jesus exhibited during his own time of trial.

We are invited to talk (pray, share stories, express hopes, weep) with one another. The best talking is done in the shadow of the Christ who always is ready to have us share at his Table—the table talk of truth and hope. Our ten pastors and their congregations needed this. In the culture at large, the conversation is often not much of a conversation. On the other hand, Jesus comes as the Word, the powerful, healing word of truth, and he invites us to share our words. It is not that our speaking is the means to minister, but the speaking *is* the work of ministry.[33]

The talk in which we are invited to participate can range from companionable silence to the storytelling that helps to organize and provide coherence to the chaotic experiences of the terminally ill. This talk helps to reconstitute the one physically broken by pain and disease and emotionally battered as a person.[34]

A *Is for Awareness*

The dying person, her or his family, and the larger church family all face a difficult transition when journeying into the reality of a terminal illness. Chapter 1 describes the drama of mutual pretense that reveals a common closed awareness that is so often chosen by people facing dying and death. The church can be a place where an open awareness of a terminal illness can be embraced. It is not the medical arena; instead there is unending space for social, spiritual, and emotional anxieties to be aired and cared for. Suffering about these issues is reduced and resilience is increased if the reality of a dying person's concerns is communicated and not suppressed or ignored.

Another layer of awareness focuses the community's communication lens on being *aware* of the messages surrounding them. So often in other life arenas, time is the enemy to

Table 3

Ideas for Facilitating Talk	Who Can Use This Idea?	What Happens with Talk?
• Communication scavenger hunt: (1) identify themes of what is and is not talked about in some aspect of the social life of the church, and (2) come together to discuss what those themes indicate.	• Christian education classes • Committee groups • Church staff	• Initiate reflexive conversation about church culture and patterns • Identify ways to change
Include dying and death as a worship component in sermon content.	• Worship committee • Church staff	• The idea of dying is included as a normative component in the language of the church.
• Create opportunities to share illness narratives within the church community (worship service, caregiver support group, bereavement support group, caregiver/congregant partnering).	• Congregants • Church staff • Outreach organizational committees	• Those suffering within the church can experience the support of others. • Overextended family and caregivers can receive support at times and in ways that are possible in the midst of their burdens.

this layer of awareness. Fortunately, the church, aware of the mandate to make the most of the time (Col. 4:5b), is not as pressed to be efficient in the ways that health-care provision is regimented. The community of faith has plenty of time for stories. Indeed, that is what the church has done for two thousand years: tell its story and hear the many stories of those in need. And such stories can heal in important ways.[35] In the faith environment, the dying person is free to "go anywhere" with her or his story, questions, complaints, or even silence. In fact, most life stories are offered without an organized plot, but rather emerge through action, deed, and relationship.

Caregivers, supporters, and friends, one's sisters and brothers in Christ, can provide attention that is not driven by their own agendas or by some preset medical or religious procedure. It has neither script nor any assumption other than care for the dying person.[36]

Jesus asked the blind man, "What do you want?" On the surface, that seems like a silly question. If Jesus knew so much, why ask a blind man what he wanted? Wouldn't he have wanted to see? But Jesus wasn't going to impose the story of the healer on the wounded whose story might have been (surprisingly) different. Instead, Jesus urged the blind man to tell his own story (Mark 10:51b). It turns out that the blind man's story, or wish, was not a surprise: "Let me see again." Even though his story was expected, it was *his* story. Jesus had an awareness of the need for each one to have his or her own space and to fill it with his or her own voiced story.

The awareness called for can be described in the words of Paul to the church at Galatia; it is an awareness characterized by other-centeredness. It is here that spirituality, a Christian spirituality, becomes palpably concrete: "the fruit of the Spirit is love, joy, peace, patience, kindness, generosity, faithfulness, gentleness, and self-control. There is no law against such things" (Gal. 5:22–23). *There is no law against such things!* Unlike the restricted administration of painkillers, the limits on chemotherapy, the haste of the visit with clinicians, or lifetime limits on insurance claims, one's patience, kindness, and gentleness can be administered without limit. The needs

Table 4

Ideas for Facilitating Awareness	Who Can Use This Idea?	What Happens with Awareness?
• Reinvigorate the prayer chain.	• Congregants	• Normalize the culture of an open awareness.
• Discuss a case study about a man with an end-stage cancer diagnosis who was afraid to share his diagnosis with anyone. Learn about his fears.	• Christian education classes • Committee groups • Church staff	• Explore the consequences of a closed awareness to terminal illness. • Brainstorm ways that church members can communicate awareness.

186

of the dying person become the criteria for the kind of care the church offers.

The ten congregations of chapter 1 seemed not to exhibit an open awareness, only misery. If they were aware of the pastor's dying, they stifled it and pretended a different story. And the ministers failed to use their doubly powerful position, as pastor *and* as dying, to address the secret fears they experienced and that their congregations held.

B *Is for the Body of Christ*

Just as the dying person suffers, so does the family and the larger community that knows that individual. Together they all share a need for community and the broad family of caregivers. A popular and perhaps useful way to view groups when cohesion and cooperation is to be emphasized is to call it a team. The president has his team of advisers, and we take our cars to highly skilled teams of mechanics. But the church is never portrayed in Scripture as a team. Instead, it is a *body*. A body is characterized by the intimate connection of each part with every other part and by the fact that each part is utterly distinct from, but absolutely necessary for the well-being of, every other part.

While a body's goal is to stay healthy, a team is out to win. While a body cannot substitute new parts for the original ones, team members can come and go. So we recognize a significant difference between what the church can provide and what a secular team of clinicians can provide.[37] Sadly, the ten pastors/churches never gave any hint that they had come together as a body, as *the* body of Christ in which they might have, together, pursued support and mutual care.

The dying person may have the medical advantage of being treated by a team of medical experts. But the dying person is not a member of that team. She or he is more like the field, pitch, or court where the game is played. If the team can't win (keep her or him alive), the team moves on to the next

187

challenge. Game over, end of (the patient's) story. Abandonment ensues.

But, again, and thankfully, the church is not a team. It is a body in which every part, every member, is connected to every other member; without a member, the body is not fully a body or fully the church. That must be a compelling conclusion for "members of the church." While the theme for a team is "go, go, fight, win," for the church it is more like the words of 2 Corinthians 1:4 about the God who "consoles us in all our affliction, so that we may be able to console those who are in any affliction with the consolation with which we ourselves are consoled by God."

Too often the dying person is eventually sloughed off of the body like a lock of hair or a toenail, gone and hardly missed. Instead, the question ought to be, what can this person, dying though he or she may be, offer the rest of the body? Rather than "team," "family" would be a better way of thinking of the church. It is not hierarchy but intimacy and connectedness that characterize the church.

From the perspective of the sick person, medical care can seem hopelessly fragmented. After waiting in a waiting room, sometimes for hours, a patient is ushered into an examination room and left to wait, perhaps with a family member or two or three in tow. Hurry up and wait. Wait for some very specialized piece of physical help that might in fact complicate other ailments. And then perhaps the patient waits some more for a referral to another doctor or clinic, or for another procedure, followed by the solitary trek from place to place. The glib affirmation of tough individualism that may have characterized life before suffers a blow. This experience can seem like a disjointed and futile quest for help that often never arrives.

We have all known or heard of stories of isolation in the midst of the crowds made up of physicians, nurses, patients, and caregivers, none of whom have been a part of our own story. And suddenly we are in their midst, yet alone. We enter and undress, not in the intimacy of our own space, but in the psychological refrigeration of an examining room.

The church is the community, the family, the social environment in which individuals who are dying can receive the comforting safety net of caring others. Occasionally the church body may be called upon for advice or direction. One writer speaks of "clearness committees"[38] by which the church can sometimes act as an aid to discernment.

Table 5

Ideas for Facilitating the Body of Christ	Who Can Use This Idea?	What Happens with the Body of Christ?
• Celebrate All Saints' Day in your church by remembering and honoring all members who died that year.	• Congregants • Church staff	• Institute a remembrance of suffering. • Continue the celebration of a life lived. • Make real and ongoing work of talking about and easing bereavement.
• Celebrate all terminally ill members and their caregivers formally each year.	• Congregants • Church staff	• Integrate the truth of dying into the life of the church. • Embrace the caregivers' burden.
• Organize several outreach ministries that include (1) food ministry, (2) transportation ministry, (3) errand ministry, and (4) respite ministry for those families facing terminal illness.	• Organizational groups within church • Multigenerational classes	• Create an outlet for caring. • Integrate key interests and strengths for congregants into the care of congregants.
• Offer caregiver skills workshops with the parish nurse, in conjunction with those congregants with nursing or other medical skills, in which procedures and techniques involved in home care can be practiced repeatedly.	• Caregivers within the church • Church staff • Skilled congregants • Church governance	• Create an outlet for caring. • Facilitate practical resolution of difficulties.

L *Is for Listening Deeply*

Rush, rush, hurry, hurry; this is the way of our culture. And in the process the dying person is too easily lost in the hustle and bustle. Take time; this is the gift that can be given to the dying. It may also be all that the dying person has left to give others. Paul exhorts us to "[make] the most of the time" (Col. 4:5b). The need being answered is the need to provide an ongoing presence and to allow the reiteration of the stories of the person dying. This does not always imply speech. It may be simply what can be described as "nonverbal immediacy."[39]

Our culture is one in which haste is expected and even admired. We are assured by television ads that "you don't have time to be sick" and are encouraged to take a pill and go on (disregarding, of course, the health hazard to others!). We are in a hurry. Even our worship, which someone has described as "wasting time with God," must be concluded in an hour so the hungry can be first to the restaurant for Sunday lunch.

When the dying leave the medical or health-care facility after a test, a procedure, or a session with the clinician, they may be in the position many of us find ourselves in after a similar meeting: "I should have asked this" or "I forgot to ask that." We wonder if we were understood by the clinicians. First it was wait, wait, and wait some more. Then it was hurry, hurry, hurry. The clinicians were on a schedule, and often, behind schedule. It was curiously, tediously hectic. And when one is very sick, it can be harder to fire up a response or deliver a clear question. So one leaves the medical environment with frustrations that may not be simply physical but also deeply personal.

In none of our conversations about the dying pastors and their congregations did we sense that deep listening was a gift granted the pastor by the congregation or requested by the pastor. From the pastors' points of view, it was largely business as usual. Receiving mindful and present listening may have been perceived as weakness and surrender, a difficult thing for Americans to acknowledge. The church can provide

Table 6

Ideas for Facilitating Listening Deeply	Who Can Use This Idea?	What Happens with Deep Listening?
• Challenge church members to allow another person to describe her or his anxiety or pain, and resist the desire to shut down her or his story by comforting or commiserating (classic tactics that end disclosure).	• Preaching staff • Church governance	• Enlarge the circle of caring.
• Keep a listening diary for a week in the church. Note the topics that were shared and how few of them addressed dying, caregiver burden, fear of death, etc.	• Church staff • Church committee structures	• Assess what the church is actually working on. • Determine who the church is caring for and who they are not.
• Practice listening in a class to a 5-minute telling of "one of life's worst moments" without verbally responding during the entire story.	• Christian education classes	• Normalize a communication skill that might be overlooked as a responsibility of the church.
• Perform a content analysis of selected hymns, prayers, or confessions identifying language about listening, illness, caring, and dying.	• Christian education classes • Worship committee	• Engage the preexisting resources that support, describe, and demonstrate deep listening in the church.

a truly different environment. It can offer a leisurely, calm, personally interested place and all the time in the world in which attention can be paid and the sufferer can be heard.

As worship has been described as "wasting time with God," so care for the dying may look to the world like wasted time. But that is the kind of time we spend with those who are dear. Time is the gift we have to give. When everyone knows what is happening, the need for truth telling forbids feverish planning of a recovery plan or diverting the conversation elsewhere to avoid the unpleasant. Instead, what is called for is deep and careful listening that acknowledges the approach of death and all of its concerns. This can embody what has been called an "ethic of consent," an attitude that does not seek to transform the world but instead to consent to God's ordering of it.[40]

In this oasis of leisure and deep listening, the church (individuals in the church would be more realistic) can absorb the sufferer's story and allow it to commingle with their own suffering. It will be one they have already heard, this time with additions, pauses, and reflections. We tell and we hear, placing the individual story within the grander narrative of the gospel that blesses and sanctifies our individual stories. And in listening, we bear one another's burdens and so fulfill "the law of Christ" (Gal. 6:2).

E *Is for Eucharist*

The celebration of the dying of Christ is an ongoing reminder to the whole church, and can be especially so to one in the valley of the shadow of dying, that the Christ is with them in their suffering. *Eucharist* is from the New Testament Greek word for "being thankful, giving thanks." Eucharist (Communion, Lord's Supper) is the rite celebrating the work of Jesus Christ—what he has done on our behalf. All we can do at this point is be thankful to be incorporated into this work of our Savior. In this celebration we recognize the brutal reality of dying and are offered the gracious opportunity to accept the gift of hope that is implicit in the resurrection of Jesus. This is where dying and death meet hope and faith, and we can emerge with renewed life in the here and now, in the church, sustained by God.

While the world is not impressed with Christian sacraments, thinking them superstition, the dying person will have returned from the medical world of "solid facts," a world in which only what can be scientifically known is real, such as the images on film, the numbers on a complete blood count, or the empirically measured discovery and growth of metastases. In that world, the nonmaterial counts for less. And yet the dying person knows about love, hope, guilt, and unfinished business, and would likely seek to address those "unreal" things if he or she had a place with which and a people with whom to engage them.

Remembering and participating in the Eucharist places us and our narratives of uncertainty, worry, and pain within that larger story of God's care for all of creation, including, specifically, each of us. At this point there is nothing for us to do but hear the truth of the story of Jesus Christ and accept God's acceptance of us.

We rejoice that we have received much. We have the treasures of Scripture and tradition that offer an understanding of living and dying that excels any other understanding attainable. We have received new insights into healthier communication in end-of-life matters. The resources we have available exceed those accessible to any previous generation. We are left with few excuses and only one real challenge: to face the end of life making the decision that is simultaneously the hardest and easiest decision of all: to trust God in Jesus Christ.

We hope we have shed some light on the church's uncertainty regarding dying and have provided resources that the church can use to strengthen that ministry so that it can truly become the "community of communication."[41] The authors have not approached this task as an academic exercise. Dying remains a profound mystery; we know no more of it than anyone else. But we have been comforted to share our "remembering" of the resources God has provided to cope with this final mystery. Our prayer is that you may also be strengthened and comforted.

"Therefore encourage one another with these words" (1 Thess. 4:18).

Discussion Questions

1. Why do you think American culture wields such power over the way Christians think and behave?

2. How might "including the dying" in the life of your church feel? How might it look to outsiders? How would it change the way your church functions?
3. What would a popular, American definition of "health" be? What is there that is true and good about it? What is there that is fundamentally false?
4. Which criterion for good dying ought to be added to the list in this chapter?

Notes

Chapter 1 The Dying Pastor

1. Mercedes Bern-Klug and Rosemary Chapin, "The Changing Demography of Death in the United States: Implications for Human Service Workers," in *End of Life Issues: Interdisciplinary and Multidimensional Perspectives*, ed. Margaret B. de Vries (New York: Springer, 1999), 265–80.

2. Joy Ufema, "Insights on Death and Dying," *Nursing* 34 (1988): 66.

3. Austin S. Babrow and Marifran Mattson, "Theorizing about Health Communication," in *Handbook of Health Communication*, ed. Teresa L. Thompson, Alicia M. Dorsey, Katherine I. Miller, and Roxanne Parrott (Mahwah, NJ: Lawrence Erlbaum, 2003), 35–61.

4. Robert Buckman, "A Practical Guide," in *Oxford Textbook of Palliative Medicine*, 2nd ed., ed. Derek Doyle, Geoffrey W. C. Hanks, and Neil MacDonald (New York: Oxford University Press, 1998), 141–58.

5. Jane Littlewood, "The Denial of Death and Rites of Passage in Contemporary Societies," in *The Sociology of Death: Theory, Culture, Practice*, ed. David Clark (Cambridge, MA: Blackwell, 1993), 69–86; see esp. 70.

6. Daniel Callahan, *The Troubled Dream of Life: In Search of a Peaceful Death* (Washington, DC: Georgetown University Press, 2000), 33.

7. Philippe Airès, *Western Attitudes toward Illness and Death*, trans. P. Ranum (Baltimore: Johns Hopkins University Press, 1974), 87–88.

8. Deborah W. Sherman, "Reciprocal Suffering: The Need to Improve Caregivers' Quality of Life through Palliative Care," *Journal of Palliative Medicine* 24, no. 4 (1998): 357–66.

9. Betty Ferrell, "Pain Management: A Moral Imperative," *American Nurses Association and the Center for Ethics and Human Rights* 5, no. 2 (1996): 4–5.

10. Ezekiel J. Emanuel, Diane L. Fairclough, Julia Slutsman, and Linda L. Emanuel, "Understanding Economic and Other Burdens of Terminal Illness:

The Experience of Patients and Their Caregivers," *Annals of Internal Medicine* 132 (2000): 451–59.

11. Barney Glaser and Anselm Strauss, *Awareness of Dying* (Piscataway, NJ: Aldine Transactions, 1965).

12. Eric Eisenberg, "Ambiguity as Strategy in Organizational Communication," *Communication Monographs* 51 (1984): 227–42.

13. Eric Eisenberg, email message to Joy V. Goldsmith, October 11, 2009.

14. Sandra Petronio, *Boundaries of Privacy: Dialectics of Disclosure* (Albany: State University of New York Press, 2002).

15. Ibid.

16. Allen Verhey, "The Practice of Prayer and Care for the Dying," in *Living Well and Dying Faithfully: Christian Practices for End-of-Life Care*, ed. John Swinton and Richard Payne (Grand Rapids: Eerdmans, 2009), 86–106.

Chapter 2 Victims of the Wrong Story

1. Alasdair MacIntyre, *After Virtue* (Notre Dame, IN: University of Notre Dame Press, 1984), 201.

2. We do not think that the pastor is more important than anyone else. Our point in focusing on the ten ministers in chapter 1 was to highlight the general failure of the churches and pastors to address death-related matters when those matters must have been so dramatically central to the lives of the churches involved.

3. References to "good dying" or "good death" should not be taken to suggest that there is a perfect or best way to face end-of-life issues. Attempts to identify a "good death" have come to many different conclusions and included many different criteria by which dying might be evaluated (see Karen E. Steinhauser, Elizabeth C. Clipp, Maya McNeilly, Nicholas A. Christakis, Lauren M. McIntyre, and James A. Tulsky, "In Search of a Good Death: Observations of Patients, Families, and Providers," *Annals of Internal Medicine* 132, no. 10 [May 16, 2000]: 825–32). We will look at a variety of criteria in chapter 8. By that time, we will have presented a number of resources from the Christian faith tradition so that the reader can examine the question of a good dying from the perspective of a Christian theology of dying.

4. James Wm. McClendon Jr., *Systematic Theology: Ethics* (Nashville: Abingdon, 1986), 143.

5. Susan Sontag, *Illness as Metaphor* (New York: Vintage, 1978), 3, distinguishes between citizenship in the land of the healthy and that in the land of the ill. Arthur W. Frank, *The Wounded Storyteller: Body, Illness, and Ethics* (Chicago: University of Chicago Press, 1995), warns of the danger that the sick and dying person's "official story" is told not by that person, but is found instead in the doctor's medical chart, allowing the person whose story it is a "narrative surrender" to alter or actually eliminate his or her own story. The difficulty of the patient's story actually being heard by the medical provider is notoriously well known. Lisa A. Cooper, Debra L. Roter, Rachel L. Johnson, Daniel E. Ford, Donald M. Steinwachs, and Neil R. Powe, "Patient-Centered Communication, Ratings of Care, and Concordance of Patient and Physician Race," *Annals of Internal Medicine* 139 (2003): 907–15,

show that physicians dominate patients in conversation at ratio of 3.22 to 0.86, meaning the clinician talks about four times as much as the patient.

That new story, the medical story, will frequently have many episodes: "Let's begin with this treatment; later we will try that treatment; if necessary, such-and-such further treatment might be considered." The framework within which episodes are offered by the doctor is one that is still that of terminality, though the patient can often hear that narrative's framework as one of hope.

6. Larry R. Churchill, "The Human Experience of Dying," *Soundings* 62 (1979): 24–37. Churchill cautions against the adequacy of employing the "stages" in Elisabeth Kübler-Ross's study of dying as efforts to urge the dying into such a procrustean bed, thus eliminating the uniqueness of each story.

7. Sherwin B. Nuland, *How We Die: Reflections on Life's Final Chapter* (New York: Alfred A. Knopf, 1994), 3.

8. Barry Bogin, *Patterns of Human Growth*, Cambridge Studies in Biological Anthropology 3 (Cambridge: Cambridge University Press, 1988), 40–41.

9. Frank, *Wounded Storyteller*, 53.

10. Vigen Guroian, "Death and Dying Well in the Orthodox Liturgical Tradition," *Second Opinion* 19, no. 1 (1993): 4, notes the force of a "secular religion" in America that demonstrates a pretense of Christianity but is non-Christian at heart.

11. While "adult" baptism in the congregational traditions and "confirmation" of baptism in the hierarchical traditions pretend to be celebrated at a point of transition to adulthood, such a view is difficult to defend in American culture. It is more likely that adult commitments, such as one's choice of and preparation for a career and selection of a life partner, occur post–high school, often in college. The argument we make about the churches' outsourcing of an understanding and a framework for care for the dying applies to the churches' outsourcing of education to the secular educational establishment.

12. Mitch Albom, *Tuesdays with Morrie: An Old Man, a Young Man, and Life's Greatest Lesson* (New York: Doubleday, 1997).

13. Randy Pausch, *The Last Lecture* (New York: Hyperion, 2008).

14. Geoffrey Gorer, "The Pornography of Death," *Encounter* 5 (October 1955): 49–52.

15. Ibid., 51. There is no contradiction here between the popular notion that all the dead will go immediately to a heavenly reward (a notion that is not a serious contender for life-shaping thought or action) and the lack of a conviction about "the bodily resurrection" of Scripture and the creeds. The funereal fantasies about Uncle Floyd fly fishing in heaven or Cousin Matilda baking her famous cookies in paradise are useful in expressing our emotions and hopes, but the prospect of death and a final judgment that evaluates the moral value of lived lives and determines an eternal destiny do not appear to be decisive in much of popular religion.

16. Ibid., 51.

17. Ibid., 52.

18. Ernest Becker, *The Denial of Death* (New York: Macmillan, 1973). The science Becker sees as most responsible is that of psychology, which promised hope by looking within the self and abandoning hope that might be founded on an external (God, etc.). When we do look for meaning outside of ourselves, Becker points out that we tend to find it in work, drugs, or shopping (172).

19. Arthur C. McGill, *Death and Life: An American Theology* (Eugene, OR: Wipf and Stock, 1987).

20. In 1990, 86.2 percent of the total adult population of the United States were church members. By 2008, that number had dropped to 76 percent. (See http://www.americanreligionsurvey-aris.org.)

21. Traditionally, significant staples of a Christian worldview—the recognition and definition of sin is a good example—have been reduced in visibility or redefined in local and often significant ways. While sin may be easily recognized in a given (local) church or denominational tradition, one would be hard pressed to find a widespread agreement on what it denotes or how significant it is. Sin and the ethical-moral dimension of Christian life to which it belongs are demonstrably not factors in any view of dying current in Christian America today. See Bonnie Miller-McLemore, "The Sting of Death," *Theology Today* 45, no. 4 (January 1989): 415–26, for one of the few treatments of the role of the ethical in the facing of death in modern times.

22. Stanley Hauerwas, "Leaving Ruins: The Gospel and Cultural Formations," in *The State of the University* (Malden, MA: Blackwell, 2007), 40.

23. Eva Jeppsson Grassman and Anna Whitaker, "End of Life and Dimensions of Civil Society: The Church of Sweden in a New Geography of Death," *Mortality* 12, no. 3 (August 2007): 261–80; see esp. 270.

24. McGill, *Death and Life*, 39.

25. Kenneth G. MacKendrick, "Intersubjectivity and the Revival of Death: Toward a Critique of Sovereign Individualism," *Critical Sociology* 31, no. 1–2 (2005): 169–83, warns against the individualism that leads people who are dying to create their own religious and spiritual death narrative.

26. Stanley Hauerwas, "How Risky Is *The Risk of Education*? Random Reflections from the American Context," in *The State of the University* (Malden, MA: Blackwell, 2007), 53.

27. The clearest example of this phenomenon is found in the hospice movement and the expanding acceptance of palliative care (medical, social, psychological, and spiritual care for the terminally ill after appropriate medical authorities have concluded that no further curative treatment is possible). By 2011, more than one million patients receive hospice care and palliative treatment per year in the United States. A typical example of contemporary end-of-life care that insists (correctly, we believe) on spiritual care is found in Mark Cobb, *The Dying Soul: Spiritual Care at the End of Life* (Philadelphia: Open University Press, 2001). This extensive introduction to the spiritual dimension of end-of-life care has virtually no substantive content when dealing with Christianity. The insistence on the need for spiritual care is there, but it is as if "spiritual" were an empty cipher awaiting content from a source yet to be determined. There are no references to Scripture or to Christ. The seven-page bibliography has no titles with obvious Christian reference. The authors of this volume do not quarrel with the hospice movement and its commitment to provide spiritual support to dying patients. What we do seek to do is to fill a noticeable gap in current "death" literature. While spirituality has come to the fore as an important dimension demanding end-of-life care, little that is substantively Christian appears to fill the category "spiritual." Our purpose is to remind the reader that the Christian tradition has very specific content at

its heart that would be important for Christians to ponder as dying becomes a looming reality. Also see Rachel Stanworth, *Recognizing Spiritual Needs in People Who Are Dying* (Oxford: Oxford University Press, 2004).

28. Christian Smith with Melinda Lundquist Denton, *Soul Searching* (Oxford: Oxford University Press, 2005), 169.

29. Tracy A. Balboni, Lauren C. Vanderwerker, Susan D. Block, M. Elizabeth Paulk, Christopher S. Lathan, John R. Peteet, and Holly G. Prigerson, "Religiousness and Spiritual Support among Advanced Cancer Patients and Associations with End-of-Life Treatment Preferences and Quality of Life," *Journal of Clinical Oncology* 25, no. 5 (2007): 555–60. See also Kevin P. Kaut, "Religion, Spirituality, and Existentialism Near the End of Life: Implications for Assessment and Application," *American Behavioral Scientist* 46, no. 2 (October 2002): 220–34. (Kaut discusses a broader concept of spirituality than a traditional, denominational, or theological one.)

30. Tony Walter, "Developments in Spiritual Care of the Dying," *Religion* 26 (1996): 353–63; see 356.

31. McGill, *Death and Life*, 19.

32. Andrea C. Phelps, Paul K. Maciejewski, Matthew Nilsson, Tracy A. Balboni, Alexi A. Wright, and M. Elizabeth Paulk, "Religious Coping and Use of Intensive Life-Prolonging Care Near Death in Patients with Advanced Cancer," *Journal of the American Medical Association* 301, no. 11 (March 18, 2009): 1140–47. In light of our expressed insistence to have personal access to the best of the inevitably limited (in both availability *and* in power) resources involved, Stanley Hauerwas notes that "the ill distribution of our health care resources . . . reflects the general inability of our society to come to terms with death" ("Finite Care in a World of Infinite Need," *Christian Scholar's Review* 38, no. 3 [2009]: 327–33; see esp. 331). McGill, *Death and Life*, 11, points out that we don't really need to pay attention to death until medical evidence shows us that it is coming. By that time, of course, it is probably too late to discuss issues such as the morality of seeking unlimited access to limited resources.

33. Karl Barth, *Church Dogmatics*, vol. 3, ed. and trans. G. W. Bromiley and T. F. Torrance (London: T&T Clark, 2009), 362.

34. John Swinton, "Why Me, Lord?," in *Living Well and Dying Faithfully: Christian Practices for End-of-Life Care*, ed. John Swinton and Richard Payne (Grand Rapids: Eerdmans, 2009), 122.

35. Frank, *Wounded Storyteller*, 77.

36. When "glorious medicine" cannot promise total victory, a step-by-step approach may be offered in which the patient is offered a small step: "Let's try this medicine (or procedure)." That is a positive statement from a trusted authority. Even if the doctor's larger narrative framework is one in which the patient will die, at least in the small-scene-by-small-scene scenario, there is hope of victory.

37. Such an interpretation is found for Isaiah 38:18–19 (where only the living, and not the dead, can praise God) in the *Holman Christian Standard Bible* (Nashville: Holman, 2009), 1187: "God benefits from keeping his saints alive. The living can praise God and they can share that praise with the following generation."

38. Charles Meyer, *Surviving Death: A Practical Guide to Caring for the Dying and Bereaved* (Mystic, CT: Twenty-Third Publications, 1991), 32, cites this as one of the death myths held by some.

39. Elisabeth Kübler-Ross, *On Death and Dying* (New York: Macmillan, 1969).

40. This poem has no title other than the first line, "Do not go gentle into that good night." It appears in numerous anthologies, including *The Norton Anthology of English Literature, Vol. 2*, 6th ed., ed. M. H. Abrams (New York: Norton, 1993), 2286.

41. It may be, of course, that behind all of the public disclosure to which we had access there were "good dyings" and positive resolutions to the stresses of the terminal illnesses. However, the knowledge we have—as it relates to the individual pastors, the congregations, and the church hierarchies involved—points to multiple dysfunctional failures of widespread and long-lasting negative impact on church life, primarily in the failure of operating a successful ministry to the terminally ill and a strengthening of that ministry through accumulated experience.

42. Richard Doss, *The Last Enemy* (New York: Harper & Row, 1974), and Karl Rahner, *On the Theology of Death* (New York: Herder & Herder, 1972), are exceptions. A lack of material in the area of caring for the needs of the dying that would aid seminarians studying to be pastors is noted by at least one seminary instructor: Karen D. Scheib, "'Make Love Your Aim': Ecclesial Practices of Care at the End of Life," in *Living Well and Dying Faithfully: Christian Practices for End-of-Life Care*, ed. John Swinton and Richard Payne (Grand Rapids: Eerdmans, 2009), 39.

Chapter 3 Jesus Christ

1. A theology of dying is what is needed. Meyer, *Surviving Death*, 75, points out that when dying/death is the subject, modern Christians focus inordinately on a "resurrection theology" that can distort a healthy Christian view of dying by minimizing dying and replacing it with poetically infantile visions of resurrection where everyone who dies will live happily ever after.

2. Cobb, *Dying Soul*, 56.

3. The message of this book is specifically directed to those who take the Christian faith seriously, especially to those who have done so for some time. Regular participation in a community (church) that shares and practices a common tradition, a part of which is preparation for and coping with dying, can be more helpful than turning in last-second desperation to some source of spiritual understanding for help (although the latter is a better alternative than never turning to it at all). The goal of this chapter is to identify specific aspects of Jesus's experience of dying that might subsequently be drawn together in a "theology of dying," a coherent set of notions that Christians may find helpful in facing end-of-life challenges. This approach to death (and dying) was called for by Richard Doss in his book *The Last Enemy*, which insisted that any "theology of death" must begin with Jesus Christ (31–32, 77). But he did not spell out, as we hope to do, the specifics of what Jesus in his life, ministry, and dying provides for the construction of a theology of dying.

4. The answer was given to a reporter by the twentieth-century theologian Karl Barth when asked what it was that he had learned in the writing of his many-volumed summary of the Christian faith.

5. Current popular notions of Christianity (and of Jesus) focus on values or on moral instruction. The first is abstract; the second, more concrete. Examples of the first might be the "value of life" or "courage in the face of death." While sounding Christian, they may not turn out to be of highest importance in the value hierarchy embodied in Jesus Christ. Examples of the second could be "Do not kill," extended to imply the imperative to maintain life at all costs. Again, this does not get us very close to understanding the Jesus whose dying occupies such a central place in Scripture and in the sacraments of the church.

6. Actually, there is little agreement on life expectancy in this period. In any case, the average life span was short by our standards. See http://www.wikipedia/wiki/User:G.W./Demography_of_the_Roman_Empire.

7. There is an ongoing debate within Christian faith on the question of whether death is a natural part of the human condition or a consequence (punishment) of human sin. If it is the latter, the human Jesus was *not* destined to die. From a practical point of view, the answer to the question does not affect our theology of dying. Regardless of the cause for death, we will still die. From a historical (political) point of view, Jesus's death was the inevitable consequence of human action, despite his own sinlessness.

8. Paul Ramsey wrote, "If the sting of death is sin, the sting of dying is solitude. . . . The chief problem of the dying is how not to die alone" (*The Patient as Person: Explorations in Medical Ethics* [New Haven: Yale University Press, 1970], 134).

9. McGill, *Death and Life*, 41.

10. Ibid., 49.

11. Ibid.

12. Ibid., 56.

13. Christians could have traditionally portrayed Christ in the same way Socrates has been portrayed: as a teacher. But we didn't. However, the danger of our seeing him primarily as a teacher is still with us. This is always worth repeating as Monika Hellwig points out in *What Are They Saying about Death and Christian Hope?* (New York: Paulist Press, 1978), 35.

14. Our thinking about the cross has become so dissociated from execution, killing, and death that millions wear crosses as decorative fashion accessories for themselves or their cars (by hanging them from the rearview mirror). At least one critic has referred to this superficialization as "Jesus on a bracelet," and another as "tee-shirt Jesus."

15. Rahner, *Theology of Death*, writes at length about how dying opens the creature to a fuller experience of the cosmos.

16. Almighty (Rev. 1:8); Alpha and Omega (Rev. 1:8; 22:13); Apostle (Heb. 3:1); Author of Life (Acts 3:15); Bread of Life (John 6:35, 41, 48); Bright Morning Star (Rev. 22:16); Christ (numerous); Cornerstone (Eph. 2:20); Faithful Witness (Rev. 1:5); Firstborn of the Dead (Rev. 1:5); Gate (John 10:7); God (John 20:28); Good Shepherd (John 10:11, 14); High Priest (Hebrews, eight times); the One Who Is, Who Was, and Who Is to Come (Rev. 1:8); Life (John 11:25); Living Bread (John

6:51); Lord (numerous); King of the Jews (Matt. 2:2; 27:37); Lamb of God (John 1:29); Master (numerous); Messiah (numerous); Passover (1 Cor. 5:7); Peace (Eph. 2:14); Pioneer and Perfecter of the faith (Heb. 12:2); Prophet (Matt. 21:11); Rabbi (John 1:49); Resurrection (John 11:25); Rock (1 Cor. 10:4); Root and Offspring of David (Rev. 22:16); Ruler of the Kings of the Earth (Rev. 1:5); Son of David (numerous); Son of God (numerous); Son of Man (numerous); Truth (John 14:6); Vine (John 15:1, 5); Way (John 14:6).

17. By the mid-fifth century (451 CE to be exact), the church had debated its way to what was to be an orthodox view on the nature of the human and the divine and the relationship of the human and divine in Jesus. He is fully divine and fully human; he is both at the same time in the same person; but there is no confusion of the two natures. While this is logically difficult if not impossible to grasp, it is an expression of the way in which Christians experience Jesus Christ.

18. M. Therese Lysaught, "Suffering in Communion with Christ: Sacraments, Dying Faithfully, and End-of-Life Care," in *Living Well and Dying Faithfully: Christian Practices for End-of-Life Care*, ed. John Swinton and Richard Payne (Grand Rapids: Eerdmans, 2009), 71.

19. Rahner, *Theology of Death*, 41, 61, 63.

20. The letters of James; 1, 2, 3 John; and Jude do not directly contribute to a theology of dying. They neither add to nor contradict anything found in the rest of the New Testament.

21. Perhaps this is the same John who authored the Gospel and the three short letters, though scholars do not agree on the author's identity since the content and style are different. Of course, if you write apocalypse, you are writing in a different genre than gospel.

22. McGill, *Death and Life*, 58.

23. Christological titles that convey some aspect of the significance of Jesus need not have their origins exclusively in Scripture. Just as Scripture gives us hundreds of instances of the title "Christ," it also offers other titles that are less frequent (popular?), such as "Pioneer and Perfecter of our faith." Post-Scripture titles have been frequent: "Lord of the Dance," "Bridge over Troubled Waters," "Man for Others," and "Great Physician." Some have been insightful; others more questionable (e.g., "World's Greatest Salesman"). While not found in Scripture in this exact form, "Lord of the Dying" seems a perfectly appropriate and useful christological title.

Chapter 4 The Difference Jesus's Dying Makes

1. Eventually, the question will arise: Did God create humans as mortals with dying programmed into the human condition from the beginning? Or did God create us to live forever, a possibility canceled out by human sin? Although Scripture seems to support the latter (Gen. 3:3), there is discussion of the question. It is not an issue for this book. The fact is, we are all destined to die. However, theologians have carried on a lively debate over the centuries, with Paul, Augustine, and Calvin agreeing that had it not been for sin, humans would not have died. Others, such as the twentieth-century theologian Karl Rahner, argued that had Adam not sinned, he would still have died; his death would have been a transition from the life of an

embodied soul into another stage of God's care. However the issue may ultimately be resolved, and however we finally understand the relationship of dying to sin, we are faced with two problems for which Christ promises answers: sin and death.

2. McGill, *Death and Life*.

3. Ibid., 83.

4. Lysaught, "Suffering in Communion," 69.

5. McGill, *Death and Life*, 94.

6. Cf. Stanworth, *Recognizing Spiritual Needs*, 78, 106.

7. Rahner, *Theology of Death*, 74.

8. McGill, *Death and Life*, 49.

9. Rahner, *Theology of Death*, 44.

10. Dietrich Bonhoeffer, *Life Together/Prayerbook of the Bible*, Dietrich Bonhoeffer Works 5 (Minneapolis: Fortress, 1996), 111–12. Emphasis added.

11. Dietrich Bonhoeffer, *Conspiracy and Imprisonment: 1940–1945*, Dietrich Bonhoeffer Works, vol. 16 (Minneapolis: Fortress, 2006), 208.

12. Rahner, *Theology of Death*, 73–74.

13. Lysaught, "Suffering in Communion," 69.

14. Rahner, *Theology of Death*, 85.

15. Frederick S. Paxton, *Christianizing Death: The Creation of a Ritual Process in Early Medieval Europe* (Ithaca, NY: Cornell University Press, 1990), 7–8.

16. Rahner, *Theology of Death*, 76.

17. Lysaught, "Suffering in Communion," 68.

18. McGill, *Death and Life*, 73.

19. Lysaught, "Suffering in Communion," 67.

20. According to Alfred C. Rush ("The Eucharist: The Sacrament of the Dying in Christian Antiquity," *Jurist* 34 [1974]: 10–35), in the Catholic tradition, the Eucharist was the sacrament for the dying. When it was offered to one who was dying, it was called the *viaticum* since it was, among other things, the food for the journey (*via*) from life through death to God. "The giving of the viaticum to one who is dying is not an individualistic rite, the private affair of this one individual; it is decidedly ecclesial in character"; that is, it became ecclesiastical because the body of Christ, offered in the Eucharist, *is* the church (33–34).

21. Peter C. Phan, *Responses to 101 Questions on Death and Eternal Life* (New York: Paulist Press, 1997).

22. Our goal is to remind the dying of what God has provided in Jesus Christ, in Scripture, and the disciplines of the church that might be sustaining at life's ending. That dying might be seen as a blessing or gift of God will seem offensive to some. That idea is not one that will seem positive to many, but it is one that has appealed to a few believers through the centuries. In days before the acceptance of Christianity as the official religion of the Roman Empire, martyrs died for their faith, viewing death as an evil lesser than capitulating to the authorities by denying their Christian faith. In the theology of death developed by Ambrose of Milan, death was good because it provided a release from the miseries of this life (David Albert Jones, *Approaching the End: A Theological Exploration of Death and Dying*, Oxford Studies in Theological Ethics [Oxford: Oxford University Press, 2007], 32). The *Larger Catechism* (Reformed Tradition), 7.195, explains why the righteous must physically die even though their sins have been forgiven: "The

righteous shall be delivered from death itself at the last day, and even in death are delivered from the sting and curse of it; so that although they die, yet it is out of God's love, to free them perfectly from sin and misery, and to make them capable of further communion with Christ in glory, which they enter upon" (Question 85). In chapter 7, among the "cloud of witnesses" to dying as a Christian, Joseph Cardinal Bernardin, *The Gift of Peace: Personal Reflections* (Chicago: Loyola Press, 1997), 135, referred to his death this way: "I look upon death as a friend, not an enemy."

23. McGill, *Death and Life*, 92.

24. Thomas G. Long, *Accompany Them with Singing: The Christian Funeral* (Louisville: Westminster John Knox, 2009), 31.

25. It is not at all our intention to disparage those who might come to Christian faith late in life. The theology of dying we find in Scripture and in the life, dying, death, and resurrection of Jesus provides a window on the possibilities of a rich life in Christ that can prepare one for end-of-life crises. This is a book written for the church, its life, its mission, and the telling of the Christian story. The message in no way should be read to imply the exclusion from the gospel story of anyone who comes to it early or late, or in ordinary or extraordinary ways.

26. Ignatius of Antioch's letter *To the Ephesians*: "you are as stones of the temple of the Father, made ready for the building of God our Father, carried up to the heights by *the engine of Jesus Christ, that is the cross*, using as a rope the Holy Spirit (9:1)." See *The Apostolic Fathers*, trans. and ed. Kirsopp Lake (Cambridge, MA: Harvard University Press, 1992), 2:183 (emphasis added).

27. "How Firm a Foundation," verse 3.

28. This passage is the scriptural basis for the anointing of the dying and for the Roman Catholic sacrament of anointing the dying.

29. Rahner, *Theology of Death*, 79.

30. McGill, *Death and Life*, 79.

31. Ibid., 92.

Chapter 5 What Do You Say to Someone Who Is Dying?

1. The Greek for "those who have died" in 4:13 is a present passive participle of the verb "to sleep," thus it could be translated as a present-tense verb as those "who are falling asleep" (i.e., "dying"). It might alternatively be an inceptive participle that could be translated as "those who are beginning to fall asleep" (i.e., "starting to die").

2. Andrew Sloan, "Lament and the Journey of Doubt," *Christian Scholars' Review* 29, no. 1 (Fall 1999): 114.

3. Verhey, "Practice of Prayer," 99.

4. Ibid., 100n7.

5. Bernardin, *Gift of Peace*, 63.

6. Churchill, "Human Experience of Dying," 34.

7. John Swinton and Richard Payne, "Introduction: Christian Practices and the Art of Dying Faithfully," in *Living Well and Dying Faithfully: Christian Practices for End-of-Life Care*, ed. John Swinton and Richard Payne (Grand Rapids: Eerdmans, 2009), 15.

8. Matthias Scharer and Bernd Jochen Hilberath, eds., *The Practice of Communicative Theology: An Introduction to a New Theological Culture* (New York: Crossroad, 2008).

9. Stanley Hauerwas, "Carving Stone or Learning to Speak Christian," in *The State of the University* (Malden, MA: Blackwell, 2007), 120, emphasis added.

10. Grassman and Whitaker, "End of Life," 272, write about end-of-life care offered by those Swedish priests and deacons regularly communing with the terminally ill and describe their language as theological and pertinent to religious and existential questions. They conclude: "Their [Christians'] language was a confident one."

Chapter 6 Preaching on Death and Dying

1. Note the almost complete failure to address dying as a topic or theme in the sermons of the ten dying pastors, as recalled by informants. So powerful is the cultural avoidance of speaking of dying that one of the authors, who filled the pulpit during the final months of life for one of the dying pastors, is reminded that he never employed issues, themes, and texts that address dying.

Chapter 7 Facing Dying Faithfully

1. Peter L. Berger, *The Sacred Canopy: Elements of a Sociological Theory of Religion* (New York: Doubleday, 1967), 45.

2. Arthur W. Frank, "The Necessity and Dangers of Illness Narratives, Especially at the End of Life," in *Narrative and Stories in Health Care: Illness, Dying, and Bereavement*, ed. Yasmin Gunaratnam and David Oliviere (Oxford: Oxford University Press, 2009), 161–75, suggests that individual narratives can be "hijacked" to serve institutional interests. In the vignettes that follow, "institutional interests" (Christian orthodoxy) remain comfortably in place while individuals use the treasury of resources in often surprisingly individualistic ways.

3. Scharer and Hilberath, eds., *Practice of Communicative Theology*, 28.

4. Churchill, "Human Experience of Dying," 33.

5. There are specific reports of Bonhoeffer's death, some of which are included. There undoubtedly are official medical reports on the deaths of O'Connor and Bernardin, which, of course, have not found their way into any publicly available publications, and might be tangentially helpful, but would ultimately be the thoughts of others, and not of the individuals at the center of our inquiry.

6. He wrote pastoral letters to six churches (Ephesus, Magnesia, Tralles, Smyrna, Philadelphia [all in what is now Turkey] and Rome) and a personal letter to Smyrna's bishop Polycarp.

7. Ign. *Eph.* 12:2; Ign. *Trall.* 13:3; Ign. *Rom.* 1:2; Ign. *Smyrn.* 11:1. The translations of this novel term range from "going to God" to "gaining God" to "achieving God." Ignatius is appropriately cautious about the specifics of heaven, the resurrection, or whatever might await him after death as a martyr. Robert Grant, *The Apostolic Fathers: A New Translation and Commentary*, The Apostolic Fathers 4 (Camden, NJ: Thomas Nelson & Sons, 1966), translates it "reach" or "attain" and comments, "To 'attain' means primarily to participate in God's new age" (43).

8. Ign. *Smyrn.* 4:2.

9. Ign. *Rom.* 4:2; Ign. *Eph.* 1:2; Ign. *Magn.* 9:1.

10. Ign. *Eph.* 3:1; Ign. *Magn.* 5:2; Ign. *Rom.* 4:1; Ign. *Trall.* 4:2; 12:3; 13:3; Ign. *Phld.* 5:1; Ign. *Smyrn.* 11:1).

11. Ign. *Rom.* 4:1–2; 6:1–3.

12. Jones, *Approaching the End*, 180, acknowledges that some may consider martyrdom as suicide. Going to one's death when there is a way out can appear to be the actions of a sick or disturbed person. Instead, as he points out, for the martyr it is an act of complete self-renunciation. The martyr does not kill himself; the martyr is killed by another. Death is willingly accepted and is a means to express love of God.

13. Ign. *Smyrn.* 5:3.

14. Ign. *Magn.* 5:2.

15. Julian of Norwich, *Showings*, trans. Edmund Colledge and James Walsh, The Classics of Western Spirituality (New York: Paulist Press, 1978).

16. Thomas à Kempis, *The Imitation of Christ*, trans. and ed. Leo Sherley-Price (London: Penguin, 1952). This book is a mystical manual of devotions often considered the foremost among all Christian books, second only to the Bible. It is a manual of instruction and spiritual guidance for the Christian life, and has been published in many languages. In it, he discusses how Jesus is the primary source for guidance in all areas of life.

17. *The Life of Venerable Marguerite Bourgeoys: Foundress of the Congregation de Notre Dame of Montreal* (New York: P. J. Kenedy & Sons, 1932), 201.

18. Ibid., 203.

19. Miguel de Unamuno, *The Tragic Sense of Life*, trans. J. E. Crawford Flitch (New York: Dover, 1921), 120. This quote of Mark 9:24 in his most well-known writing (first published in 1913) captures Unamuno's tortured struggles. The "tragic sense of life" is that sense of despair and hope that humans have when they realize that life will ultimately be confronted with the reality of dying.

20. Miguel de Unamuno, *The Christ of Velázquez: A Poem*, trans. Jaime R. Vidal (Quincy, IL: Franciscan Press, 1999). The Christ at the focus of Unamuno's thoughts is the Jesus who is portrayed in a painting by Diego Velásquez in about 1632. It is a full-frontal portrait of the near-naked Jesus stretched out and (perhaps?) dead on the cross. The flesh-colored body hangs in striking contrast to the black background. It is quite physically sensual. While it may seem unusual for a portrait to provide end-of-life solace, the use of art, music, poetry, and other fine arts is occasionally found to be quite helpful.

21. Ibid., 101.

22. Ibid., 25.

23. Ibid., 82.

24. Ibid., 73.

25. Miguel de Unamuno, *The Christ of Velázquez*, trans. Eleanor L. Turnbull (Baltimore: Johns Hopkins Press, 1951), 119.

26. Although he never moves on to the resurrection, it is of some interest. If there is a resurrection, he felt it must be a resurrection of the whole man so that the individual is preserved. But it could not be an experience devoid of that tragic sense in which tension and conflict mark life. The popular image of resurrection,

described by one writer as simply a "change of horses," where we continue our earthly lives, except more comfortably, would be a horror for Unamuno, who could not envision existence without conflict or at least tension. He is not alone in such unorthodox thinking about whatever postmortem experience awaits us. McGill, *Death and Life*, wrote that he was not interested in the popular vision of heaven "where we possess ourselves and live for ourselves." That would be "a place of intolerable boredom" (70). Instead, McGill foresees something "rich in self expenditure and . . . the giving up of life for others . . . of course, life will be restored by God—for death is simply, in this perspective, the essential condition of need in which we wait upon God to give us ourselves" (80).

27. Dietrich Bonhoeffer, *Letters and Papers from Prison*, enl. ed., ed. Eberhard Bethge (New York: Simon & Schuster, 1997), 371.

28. Dietrich Bonhoeffer, *Ethics*, ed. Eberhard Bethge (New York: Macmillan, 1964), 16. That moderns make an idol of death is central to Rahner (*Theology of Death*) and McGill (*Death and Life*).

29. Bonhoeffer, *Ethics*, 17.

30. Bonhoeffer, *Letters and Papers*, 381.

31. Ibid., 16.

32. Eberhard Bethge, *Dietrich Bonhoeffer: Theologian, Christian, Man for His Times: A Biography* (Minneapolis: Fortress, 2000), 927.

33. For example, in Dietrich Bonhoeffer, *Conspiracy and Imprisonment: 1940–1945*, Dietrich Bonhoeffer Works, vol. 16 (Minneapolis: Fortress, 1996), 163, he admits that "the question of what has lasting existence in the face of death won't let me go."

34. Bonhoeffer, *Life Together/Prayerbook*, 176.

35. Bonhoeffer, *Conspiracy and Imprisonment*, 161.

36. Andrew Chandler, "The Death of Dietrich Bonhoeffer," *Journal of Ecclesiastical History* 45 (1994): 448–59.

37. Sally Fitzgerald, *Flannery O'Connor: The Habit of Being* (New York: Farrar, Straus & Giroux, 1979), 577. O'Connor's correspondence was voluminous. In this letter to a friend—written less than three months before her death, and largely about the personal and mundane aspects of their relationship—she cryptically mentions a Mass to be offered "for my intentions." She writes that she doesn't know what her intentions are, but that "whatever suits the Lord suits me."

38. Ibid., 90.

39. Ibid., 509.

40. Ibid., 163.

41. Ibid., 520, 527.

42. Ibid., 591.

43. Penny Lernoux, *Cry of the People: The Struggle for Human Rights in Latin America: United States Involvement in the Rise of Fascism, Torture, and Murder and the Persecution of the Catholic Church in Latin America* (Garden City, NY: Doubleday, 1980).

44. John F. Kavanaugh, *Faces of Poverty, Faces of Christ* (Maryknoll, NY: Orbis Books, 1991).

45. Bernardin, *Gift of Peace*, 75. A self-description Bernardin uses as a heading to part 3 of this book.

46. Ibid., 81.

47. Ibid., 132.

48. Ibid., 126.

49. Ibid., 63, 94.

50. Ibid., 94.

51. Ibid., 135.

52. Lysaught, "Suffering in Communion," 77–82.

53. Bernardin, *Gift of Peace*, 126.

Chapter 8 A Good Dying

1. There still is no dictionary definition for a good dying. We have reminded the reader of resources that the Christian faith provides for us that change our lives and prepare us for all challenges. In this chapter we will continue to mine the treasures of the traditions of the past in order to place more resources within the reach of those coping with dying today. We will conclude the book with some suggestions that communication specialists have found are most helpful in enabling the sick and the caring to make the work of dying as victorious for the Christian as possible.

2. Abigail Rian Evans, "Healing in the Midst of Dying: A Collaborative Approach to End-of-Life Care," in *Living Well and Dying Faithfully: Christian Practices for End-of-Life Care*, ed. John Swinton and Richard Payne (Grand Rapids: Eerdmans, 2009), 169.

3. Douglas C. Smith and Michael F. Maher, "Healthy Death," *Counseling and Values* 36, no. 1 (October 1991): 42–48.

4. Jones, *Approaching the End*, 219. Jones focuses on the "theology of death" gleaned from four theologians: Saint Ambrose, Saint Augustine, Saint Thomas Aquinas, and Karl Rahner.

5. David Cassarett and Sharon Inouye, "Diagnosis and Management of Delirium Near the End of Life," *Annals of Internal Medicine* 135 (2001): 32–40; and Rebecca Sudore, P. Villars, and E. Carey, "Sitting with Your Suffering: Lessons about Intractable Pain at the End of Life," *Journal of Palliative Medicine* 13 (2010): 779–82.

6. Guenter B. Risse, *Mending Bodies, Saving Souls: A History of Hospitals* (New York: Oxford University Press, 1999).

7. Deborah McBride, "End-of-Life Conversations Reduce Costs in Final Weeks of Life," *Oncology Nurse Forum* 23 (2008): 6–12.

8. Kara Zivin Bambauer, Baohui Zhang, Paul K. Maciejewski, Neayka Sahay, William F. Pirl, Susan D. Block, and Holly G. Prigerson, "Mutuality and Specificity of Mental Disorders in Advanced Cancer Patients and Caregivers," *Social Psychiatry and Psychiatric Epidemiology* 41 (2006): 819–24.

9. Greer Donley and Marion Danis, "Making the Case for Talking to Patients about the Costs of End-of-Life Care," *Journal of Law, Medicine, and Ethics* 39 (2011): 183–93.

10. Sandra L. Ragan, Elaine M. Wittenberg-Lyles, Joy Goldsmith, and Sandra Sanchez-Reilly, *Communication as Comfort: Multiple Voices in Palliative Care* (New York: Routledge, 2008), 56, 65–66, 68–70, 78, 81, 107.

11. Phelps et al., "Religious Coping," 1140–47.

12. Many of these questions are not simply about a single terminally ill person. But such broader issues ought to also be discussed in the church. The needs of the sick are infinite. How much *total* care is available for the unending needs? The number of doctors, nurses, antibiotics, therapies, hospital beds, etc., is finite. Why should (American) Christians who can afford enormous amounts of care be privileged in their access to a finite resource when the need for care is infinite? Frankly facing such questions may be something that the church can eventually embrace as part of its end-of-life ministry. Stanley Hauerwas raises this issue in "Finite Care in a World of Infinite Need," *Christian Scholars' Review* 38, no. 3 (Spring 2009): 327–33, and extensively quotes Ramsey, *Patient as Person*, 239–40.

13. Ramsey, *Patient as Person*, 113.

14. Ibid., 134.

15. Sherry Weitzen, Joan M. Teno, Mary Fennell, and Vincent Mor, "Factors Associated with Site of Death: A National Study of Where People Die," *Medical Care* 41 (2003): 323–35.

16. Hauerwas reminds us that the sick are not called "patients" for no reason. Perhaps the only available resource on the practice of Christian virtues as they relate to dying is that of John Swinton and Richard Payne, eds., *Living Well and Dying Faithfully: Christian Practices for End-of-Life Care* (Grand Rapids: Eerdmans, 2009).

17. Organ donation is another action that the dying can offer. Abigail Rian Evans, *Is God Still at the Bedside? The Medical, Ethical, and Pastoral Issues of Death and Dying* (Grand Rapids: Eerdmans, 2011), 177.

18. From W. B. Yeats's poem "The Second Coming," in *The Norton Anthology of English Literature, Vol. 2*, 6th ed., ed. M. H. Abrams (New York: Norton, 1993), 1880–81.

19. Rahner, *Theology of Death*, 31.

20. Guroian, "Death and Dying Well," 10.

21. Mary M. Doornbos, Ruth E. Groenhout, and Kendra G. Hotz, *Transforming Care: A Christian Vision of Nursing Practice* (Grand Rapids: Eerdmans, 2005), 56.

22. Smith and Maher, "Healthy Death," 4. See also Frank, *Wounded Storyteller*, 115–36.

23. Alexis Tomarken, Jimmie Holland, Sherry Schachter, Lauren Vanderwerker, Enid Zuckerman, Christian Nelson, Elliot Coups, Paul Michael Ramirez, and Holly Prigerson, "Factors of Complicated Grief Pre-Death in Caregivers of Cancer Patients," *Psycho-Oncology* 17, no. 2 (2008): 105–11.

24. One of the authors reports the following experience: "When a loved one had been suddenly struck down with a terminal illness, I approached my pastor with the 'why' question. The pastor was accommodating and spent quite a long while discoursing on death, which I found comforting. Looking back on what he said, I can't remember the content, which was not, finally, convincing, but I do remember the comfort I received in his attention to the question. Later, I was called upon to try to 'explain' the same person's death to another relative. By that time I had developed a rational 'explanation' that I have used many times. I have found it convincing—but always for only a few minutes. Then the 'explanation' disintegrates, and the 'why' question returns. But the question and the grief could at least be held at bay momentarily. There was comfort in talking it through."

25. Miller-McLemore, "The Sting of Death," 420.

26. Ibid., 421.

27. Ibid., 422.

28. Ramsey, *Patient as Person*, 113.

29. Eva Grunfeld, Doug Coyle, Timothy Whelan, Jennifer Clinch, Leonard Reyno, Craig C. Earle, Andrew Willan, Raymond Viola, Marjorie Coristine, Teresa Janz, and Robert Glossop, "Family Caregiver Burden: Results of a Longitudinal Study of Breast Cancer Patients and Their Principal Caregivers," *Canadian Medical Association Journal* 170, no. 12 (June 8, 2004): 1795–1801.

30. "A word (as *NATO, radar, or snafu*) formed from the initial letter or letters of each of the successive parts or major parts of a compound term" (*Webster's New Collegiate Dictionary* [Springfield, MA: Merriam, 1975], s.v. "acronym").

31. Elaine Wittenberg-Lyles, Joy Goldsmith, Sandra Ragan, and Sandra Sanchez-Reilly, *Dying with Comfort* (Cresskill, NJ: Hampton Press, 2010).

32. Cf. uses of prayer to maneuver God to heal in chapter 2.

33. Cf. Hauerwas, "Carving Stone," 120.

34. Arthur W. Frank, "The Necessity and Dangers of Illness Narratives, Especially at the End of Life," in *Narrative and Stories in Health Care: Illness, Dying, and Bereavement*, ed. Yasmin Gunaratnam and David Oliviere (Oxford: Oxford University Press, 2009), 161–75.

35. Frank, "Necessity and Dangers of Illness Narratives," 161–75.

36. Wittenberg-Lyles et al., *Dying with Comfort*, 255. Case studies in which chaplains or hospice caregivers report on individual deaths tend to focus on one issue (perhaps abandonment or guilt or a broken relationship). They do not depict dying persons as afflicted with numerous end-of-life concerns and an abundance of unanswered questions or tasks to be completed. The caregiver (professional, personal friend, or family member) needs to be particularly attentive to that one thing and not worry about checking to see if the dying person has any of the wide range of other possible end-of-life concerns. See also the range of various concerns in William H. Griffith's *More Than a Parting Prayer: Lessons in Care-Giving for the Dying* (Valley Forge, PA: Judson Press, 2004).

37. While this is *not* a criticism of what is currently generally on offer from the techno-medical world of health care, it is hoped that professional caregivers will continue to improve in the matter of patient-centered care. See Wittenberg-Lyles et al., *Dying with Comfort*.

38. Scheib, "'Make Love Your Aim,'" 30–56; see esp. 53.

39. Wittenberg-Lyles et al., *Dying with Comfort*, 252.

40. Doornbos, Groenhout, and Hotz, *Transforming Care*, 26.

41. Scharer and Hilberath, eds., *Practice of Communicative Theology*.

Subject Index

abandonment, 49, 66–67, 103, 116, 169
  by clinician, 168, 188
America
  culture of dying in, 3, 10, 17, 19, 27–30,
    33, 38–39, 43–45, 179
  as hoping in science to deny death, 2,
    10, 41
  religiosity in, 2, 26, 32–34, 123, 197n10
  and secular story of dying, 25–26, 30,
    33, 41, 45, 100, 183
  values in, 32, 33, 39, 171, 172, 179, 188,
    209n12
ars moriendi. See Art of Dying, The
Art of Dying, The, xvii–xviii, 140
attitudes toward dying
  acceptance, 45, 66, 103, 118, 146, 165,
    179, 193
  avoidance, 2–4, 7, 9, 18, 50, 115, 181,
    205n1
  denial, 1, 4, 9, 10, 12, 14, 21, 22, 44, 48,
    83, 114, 132, 181

baptism, x–xi, 86–93, 167, 168, 170, 174,
  177
  corporate, 48, 86, 92
  dying in, 75, 81, 86–89, 100, 103, 148,
    172, 173
  as signifying transformation, 81, 87–90,
    104, 119

beatitudes for the dying, 167, 168, 170,
  174–77
Bernardin, Joseph Cardinal, 118, 158–60
Bible. *See* Scripture
Bonhoeffer, Dietrich, 152–55
Bourgeoys, Marguerite, 149–50

caregiver/caregiving/caring, 118, 167–69,
  174, 179–80, 185–87, 189, 191,
  210nn36
  "only caring," 169, 179–80
Christians
  acquainted with death, xviii, 107, 131
  already having died in Christ, xix, 99
  identity as, 92–93, 103
    acquainted with dying, 99, 131–32
    aliens, 90, 99, 102, 169
    body of Christ, 94–95, 137
    citizens of heaven, 99
    community, 145, 153–54
    community of communication, xix,
      119, 193
    earthen vessels, 99
    exiles, 90, 99, 102, 169
    as family, 17, 93–94, 159, 169, 170,
      184, 188, 189
    image of God, 65, 103–4
    raised to new life in Christ, xvii, 99
    sojourners, 99

Author Index

215

Scripture Index

Note: Page numbers in **boldface type** indicate a quotation of the verse or verses cited.